YOU ARE ALWAYS WITH ME

YOU ARE ALWAYS WITH ME
LETTERS TO MAMA 1923–1932
FRIDA KAHLO

EDITED, TRANSLATED AND INTRODUCED BY HÉCTOR JAIMES

Peace doesn't fight for itself
You have to work hard to
keep it. x x x

virago

VIRAGO

First published in Great Britain in 2018
by Virago Press

1 3 5 7 9 10 8 6 4 2

A CIP catalogue record for this book
is available from the British Library.

ISBN 978-0-349-01195-0

Design by Andrew Barron
Printed and bound in Italy by L.E.G.O. SpA

Papers used by Virago are from
well-managed forests
and other responsible sources.

Virago Press
An imprint of
Little, Brown Book Group
Carmelite House
50 Victoria Embankment
London EC4Y 0DZ

An Hachette UK Company
www.hachette.co.uk

www.virago.co.uk

CONTENTS

INTRODUCTION

FRIDA KAHLO TOOK HERSELF AS HER SUBJECT. HER IMAGE, HER POSITION in the painting – in a landscape or with people – is always the heart of the matter.

Since her first portrait in 1927 at the age of twenty, *Self-Portrait in a Velvet Dress* (p. 11), we see that she uses herself to represent a mood, a feeling, a truth; in essence, her sense of herself. Frida's gaze, under her famous brow, is bold and reinforced by the intensity of the colour of her burgundy dress and the tempestuous blue background.

She wrote in her diary: 'La revolución es la armonía de la forma y del color. Y todo está, y se mueve, bajo una sola ley: la vida. Nada está aparte de nadie. Nadie lucha por sí mismo. Todo es todo y uno. La angustia y el dolor; el placer y la muerte, no son más que un proceso para existir. La lucha revolucioinaria en este proceso es una puerta abierta a la inteligencia.'

'Revolution is the harmony of form and colour. And everything remains and moves under one law: life. No one is apart from anybody. Nobody struggles on his own. All is everything and one. Anguish and pain; pleasure and death, are nothing but a way to exist. In this process, the revolutionary struggle is an open door to intelligence.'

As a child she suffered polio and when she was an adolescent she suffered a terrible traffic accident which resulted in psychological and physical trauma that was to remain for the rest of her life. Without a doubt these events – as well as her tumultuous relationship and marriage to the Mexican mural painter Diego Rivera – influenced her artistic vision.

If her paintings question identity, they also show the universality of pain and of suffering that derives from the human experience. By becoming her own artistic object Frida Kahlo transforms herself as much as she does us, as viewers. This may be why her life and art have such a

ILLUSTRATION ON PAGES 6–7
Frida's parents, Guillermo Kahlo and Matilde Calderón when young.

YOU ARE ALWAYS WITH ME

capacity to win followers of diverse backgrounds; despite producing paintings that were often uncomfortable because of their violent and cruel content, we can see and feel commonalities.

Frida wrote, 'There have been two great accidents in my life. One was the streetcar, and the other was Diego. Diego was by far the worst.' These have been the usual reference points from which to interpret her work, alongside her eccentric life, but there is much to indicate that even in her youth she displayed a restless, uncommon, creative and defiant personality.

In her diary, for example, there is not a daily or even intermittent narration of her memories or experiences but rather a non-chronological accumulation of sketches, drawings, strokes, ideas, poems and writings.

As well as keeping her diary, Frida wrote letters: a copious number to her friends, to Diego, to her doctor and to her lovers. Some of these have been published and show the woman, the wife, the lover and the artist she was.

However, until now these letters to her beloved mother, Matilde Calderón Kahlo, have not been collected and published in English.

The woman who is now recognised as one of Mexico's greatest painters was born on 6th July 1907 in Coyoacán, the third of four daughters, to a mestizo woman (of Spanish/Indian descent) and a German father, Wilhelm Kahlo, who had changed his name to Guillermo Kahlo when he had arrived in Mexico as a young man. Thanks to his wife's father, he had learned photography and at the time of the birth of Frieda – spelt the German way until she changed it herself later – was making his living as a professional photographer. Though Frida loved her father, she was close to her mother – a fact amply demonstrated by this wonderful, brief collection of letters she wrote to her dear Mama between 1923 and her mother's death in 1932.

OPPOSITE
*Self-Portrait in a Velvet
Dress,* 1927
(oil on canvas)

Frida Kahlo has become the subject of study from the perspectives of feminism, Marxism, psychoanalysis, cultural studies, sociology, art history, photography, fashion and even literature. Her work has become universal in the truest sense of the word; a universality not attained solely through her painting or her clothes or photographs but rather through the aesthetic of her life's work – including her letters.

Diego Rivera, the great painter and muralist, was her mentor, her friend and her husband. But Frida learned to distance herself from his influences and developed and created her own singular style. In Diego's Mexican period we see a wide array of historical representations of society, such as in the murals at the Secretariat of Public Education, Chapingo University or at the National Palace. Frida's works, however, are timeless. Her art, unlike her husband's, does not have a beginning or an end; hers privileges a view of the senses. It is interesting to me that Diego features Frida in his paintings as a revolutionary in arms and not, as I think of her, as a revolutionary of art. That revolutionary artistic drive and timelessness is why Kahlo has emerged the more famous artist since their deaths.

Surrealism has been the school of art with which Frida Kahlo's works have been most commonly associated, and even though we can find some of its traits in her works – she did use symbolism and allegory to transform reality – her art surpasses that classification. The 'father of Surrealism', André Breton was fascinated by Frida's paintings, but his theories made her feel uncomfortable. To my mind, in the paintings by the other Mexican women painters associated with Surrealism, such as María Izquierdo, Rosa Rolanda, Remedios Varo and Leonora Carrington, the imaginary universe seems to take control of their paintings, while Frida Kahlo's paintings invoke a deeply personal experience.

" Don't be sad, because I am doing very well, Diego is very kind to me and besides, I will heal better here than in Mexico.

The archives at the Frida Kahlo Museum in Mexico City contain a large number of notes, notebooks and letters, among other materials that Frida accumulated throughout her life; from these I have selected the first eleven letters, beginning when she was aged sixteen, two years prior to her accident. She was writing to her mother when she was at school in Mexico City, eleven kilometres from her home. The other set of letters, from the archives at the National Museum of Women in the Arts in Washington, DC, were written after she was married at the age of twenty-two, when she travelled with Diego Rivera to the United States. He had been commissioned to paint murals in San Francisco (*Allegory of California* and *The Making of a Fresco*) and then later in New York; only one letter was written while Frida was still in Mexico.

The trip to San Francisco was the first time Frida had travelled abroad, and importantly it was where she met the doctor who treated her for the terrible pain sustained by her injuries. Her letters to Dr Leo Eloesser indicate that a very close relationship developed over the years he cared for her.[1] San Francisco is also where, for the first time, Frida seriously took up painting.

The Mexican letters here show the playfulness and affection of a young girl and introduce Diego Rivera, of whom Frida seems perhaps slightly in awe. Then there is a gap: on 17th September 1925, the bus she was travelling on was struck by a streetcar, leaving the eighteen-year-old Frida with a broken spine and smashed pelvic bone; her injuries were so severe that doctors did not expect her to survive. In May 1927 we see the beginning of one of the constant refrains of these letters, her health: 'Dearly precious Mama, Don't worry about me, because I have been well, Maty [her sister] already took me to see the Dr and tomorrow they will set my cast, here at Maty's house. I will tell you later how much it cost; you'll see if you can contribute with something, don't you think?'

1
See, Querido Doctorcito: Frida Kahlo–Leo Eloesser, correspondencia (México, DGE Equilibrista/ Conaculta, 2007).

In August 1929 she became Diego Rivera's third wife. Their ages – he was forty-two, she was twenty-two – were not the only vastly different things about them, as shown in Frida's 1931 painting, *Frida and Diego Rivera* (p.111).

The next group of letters (from San Francisco and New York) shows her relationship with her mother as deep and intense; the almost obsessive attachment revealed by these letters would continue until Frida's mother died aged fifty-eight, when Frida was just twenty-five. The letters express a constant wish and anxiety: to be close to her mother and to make sure that she and the family were managing. Frida's depiction of her mother in the painting she completed after her mother's death, *My Grandparents, My Parents and Me* (1936) (pp.16–17), confirms the central role she played. This painting portrays what appears to be a family tree, but its branches have been replaced by a ribbon of blood that Frida, as a girl, holds. Her grandparents appear in a parallel fashion on each side of the painting but her mother is dominant and gazing directly at the viewer.

In her letters Frida writes as if she is speaking – she omits punctuation marks or doesn't use them properly; often she doesn't, as one should in Spanish, open or close the question and exclamation marks. She doesn't seem to know how to distinguish between a full stop followed by a phrase or one followed by a new paragraph; and she makes many spelling mistakes. Although most of these errors have been corrected in the English version for clarity, what I see in Frida's writing is similar to her painting: sensations that turn the pages into a painter's palette.

In San Francisco she was dramatically affected by loneliness while Diego was away painting, and sadness at being far away from her mother; paradoxically, this solitude – above anything else – motivated her to continue painting. We read: 'You have no idea how much I miss you, and I don't stop thinking of you, not even for a moment. I am painting and that way I get some distraction, because otherwise I would be terribly bored.'

The other recurring theme was money – or the lack of it. Her father was unemployed at this point and Frida felt an obligation to help out financially; turning to painting was also a means to help them. 'I hope I can sell some paintings so that I can send you money, because my greatest fear is that you won't have enough money, and I'll never hear about it.'

She was appalled by the divide between the rich and the poor in America. 'There are three thousand Mexicans in Los Angeles who have to work like mules to compete in business with the gringos.' From this experience Frida painted *Self-Portrait Along the Borderline Between Mexico and the United States* (1932) (pp.88–9), in which Frida's figure appears in the foreground, in the middle of the painting, as if it were divided into two sections. The upright position of her body in an incongruously pink dress, with her fixed gaze and look of bewilderment, demonstrates tension. Her left hand, which points to Mexico, holds the Mexican flag; in her right hand, which points to the United States, she holds a cigarette. She is implying her distance from both worlds: the Mexican side is a lifeless, mythic past, and the American side with its industrialised present, is cold and inhumane.

Frida never felt comfortable in the United States, as these letters reiterate over and over again, and what we also see here is her stark awareness of being different: an object of curiosity. 'The gringas have liked me very much and they are impressed by the dresses and the shawls that I brought with me, my jade necklaces are amazing to them and all the painters want me to pose for their portraits; they are a bit naive, but very good people.'

Frida's paintings seem to pull us towards her, in her direction, to her centre, but her presence, visible and invisible, remains a medium of

"
I hope I can sell some paintings so that I can send you money, because my greatest fear is that you won't have enough money, and I'll never hear about it.

transit – changing experience through perception, sensation and reflection. And to me, just as with her paintings, Frida was trying to capture a sense of transitional worlds. With each letter she was trying to hold to herself the world of her family through the overflowing love she poured out to her mother. 'Aunque ahora estamos tan lejos tú siempre estás conmigo en todas partes.' 'Although we are now so far away from each other, you are always with me everywhere I go.' This maternal love was fixed and constant for her; everything else – the ability to have a child herself, good health and a stable relationship – seemed beyond her reach.

But perhaps it's through this love that we are able to know Frida Kahlo a bit more.

She is the painter who is already part of us; we recognise ourselves in her.

HÉCTOR JAIMES

My Grandparents, My Parents and Me, 1936
(oil on board)

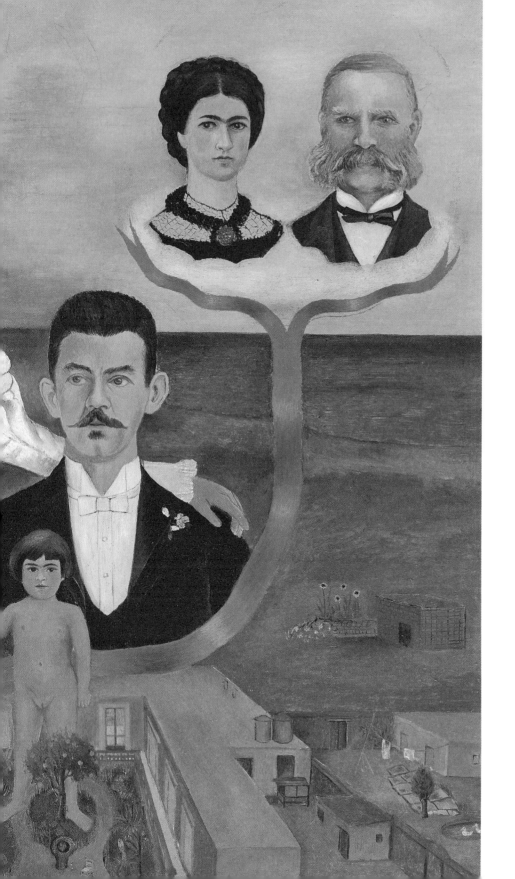

MEXICO

FRIDA TRAVELLED FROM HER HOME IN COYOACÁN TO MEXICO CITY, where her school, Escuela Nacional Preparatoria, was located. At that time the school had two thousand students, only thirty-five of whom were female. From there, aged sixteen, she wrote her mother these few schoolgirl letters, asking for permission, for example, to stay and hear a talk by Diego Rivera. We also see her slightly mischievous behaviour.

In 1923, just three years after the decade in which the Mexican Revolution took place, President Álvaro Obregón had managed to achieve relative peace. He is remembered for the educational and cultural transformations that occurred during his administration; he created the 'Secretaría de Educación Pública' (Secretariat of Public Education) and appointed the philosopher José Vasconcelos as its director. Vasconcelos extended public education throughout the country and invited several prominent painters to paint murals with cultural and national themes on the walls of public buildings, thus giving birth to the Mexican muralist movement.

Having spent almost fourteen years in Europe, Diego Rivera returned to Mexico and embraced the muralist movement. The year before Frida's first letter, in 1922, he finished his first Mexican mural, *Creation*, in the Simon Bólívar theatre at Frida's school.

ILLUSTRATION ON
PAGES 18–19
Frida's mother with her family. A bold and playful Frida is wearing a three-piece suit and holding a cane.

YOU ARE ALWAYS WITH ME

The year 1922 was significant because Diego Rivera joined the Mexican Communist party, and although his first mural did not reflect a communist ideology, this was to change in his later commissions, including those for the Secretariat of Public Education building, Chapingo University and the National Palace.

After her accident at eighteen, we have a letter written in 1927, when Frida had moved in with her sister Matilde Kahlo (Maty), where she talks of her health and tries to persuade her mother things are going well.

By 1930, the date of the last letter in this section, she is married to Diego.

These defining moments – her accident and marriage – I see in her painting *The Bus* (1929) (pp.30–1), which shows an array of characters of different social classes, and demonstrates a more committed political awareness, thanks to her association with Diego, and a peaceful bus trip, perhaps depicting how things could have been.

YOU ARE ALWAYS WITH ME

I

Dear Mama

Today I will stay at school because Diego Rivera will deliver a lecture and I believe it's about Russia and I would like to learn some about Russia. If you would like to come, let me know at noon, tell the servant so that I wait for you. Today I have behaved well and I have not missed a class.

Send me five cents for an ice cream cone and five cents for quesadillas.

Your daughter
Frieda[2]

Diego Rivera will start speaking at eight in the amphitheatre; don't miss it, dear Mama.

2
Frida's father was originally from Germany, and she signed her name in the German way: Frieda.

OPPOSITE
A studio photograph of Frida dated 1926, probably taken on a trip to Mexico City.

2

10th May 1923

Dear Mama

Mrs Castillo[3] sends you this little piece of paper, along with this carnation.

   We did have class this morning but I do not know if they will let us go in the afternoon, they haven't told us anything yet, there is going to be a huge party and I think we will also have class, who knows. Well dear Mama, when they come to get me send me five cents for an ice cream cone; I beg you, don't forget it.

Your daughter who loves you
Frieda

My father says not to worry for him as he is now going to arrive later.

3
The school's prefect.

3

Dear Mama

Please have your anger go away, and listen to what I am going to tell you: I will go with Maty[4] to the Legation immediately, because my father is furious and he doesn't want to listen to anything; it's best for him not to see the Dieners[5] because otherwise the whole thing will fall apart. If you'd like I will go and get you this afternoon so that we can see them, as Maty can't come with me because Fil Pagasa will go to her house for lunch, plus she is not too interested in the issue. After I eat I will go to the office and get the message you will convey with Aureliano. I can't do anything like that by myself so you and I have to agree, without getting angry or anything because otherwise the devil will take us away. I am going to go with G. Arias[6] to court to see how the issue with my father is going and to see if it's possible to transfer the foreclosure[7] to Mexico as soon as possible.

Let me know if I should come and get you this afternoon or not.

Nothing can be arranged with my father.

Your daughter
Frieda

You have to understand that unfortunately in situations like these, one depends on other people, and one has to bear the fact that they will learn about everything. I am going to eat with Maty, don't send me food.

4
Matilde Kahlo, Frida's sister.
5
The Diener family owned La Perla, the jewellery store where Guillermo Kahlo set up his photography studio, which was located in downtown Mexico City, very close to the Escuela Nacional Preparatoria.
6
Alejandro Gómez Arias, Frida's boyfriend, for whom she painted *Portrait of Alejandro Gómez Arias* (1928).
7
In 1912 the Kahlos had to mortgage their house, and Frida is probably talking about the foreclosure on their home.

4

Dear Mama

I met Alberto Landa and he asked me to come and see him because otherwise he will not be liable for my tooth, so tonight, when I get to Coyoacán I am going to see him, all right? Please tell Máximo to wait for me at the corner between Presidencia street and Mrs Inés's coalyard. I will come back to town at seven or seven-thirty and I will leave Alberto's house at eight, at the latest, so I'll be home at around quarter-past eight. I already asked about the shawl. It costs $3.00, of very good quality.

I will send you the one I found; they didn't have it in another colour.

As I didn't have enough money, I was not able to buy you the pins, but please be a little patient and I will buy them for you.

Your daughter who loves you dearly
Frieda

" You and I have to agree without getting angry or anything, because otherwise the devil will take us away.

5

Dear Mama

My father left because he still has vertigo, but I will stay to resolve the issue with the Ministry of Industry and see Salomón and the gentleman of the 'City of London', so send me food and I'll come back in the afternoon.

Adriana[8] says that Guero[9] maybe wants two simple shirts instead.

Your daughter who loves you
little Frieda

8
Adriana Kahlo, Frida's sister.
9
Alberto Veraza, Adriana Kahlo's husband. 'Guero' was his nickname.

6

Precious Mama

At the end I will go with Guero at six, so I don't know at what time I will arrive; when my father comes home he is going to ask you if it's true that you asked me for a photograph of one of the paintings that 'Dilubio' gave you; tell him that you did, because if you tell on me I will get upset, all right? Don't be unkind because I wanted it for me, and he caught me right there, and I had no choice but to tell him a lie. He will tell you that he had already brought it to you, but you tell him that you didn't remember.

Your daughter who loves you
Frieda

Dear Mama, read it before my father starts talking to you.

7

Precious Mama

Máximo arrived at a very good time; my father's mood is so so.

I have almost finished eating, so if the little gringo arrives before I get there, please tell him to wait for me, with the excuse that I was supposedly still eating in Mexico,[10] all right? Please do me that favour, because we are going to swim at Rocha's house and to play chess a little bit.

Is Kitty[11] less angry now?

Your daughter who loves you
Frieda

[10]
Mexico City.
[11]
Cristina Kahlo, Frida's sister. Her nickname was 'Kitty'.

The Bus, 1929 (oil on board)

YOU ARE ALWAYS WITH ME

8

15th August 1923

Mama

Tomorrow's conference will take place now and that's why I will arrive at eight-thirty or nine.

I went to mass at eight in the morning and I saw Miss Lebrós, who says hello to you and to Grandma[12] as well.

That poet who wrote to me gave me a very pretty book, here is the little card and tonight I will show you the book.

Your daughter who loves you
Frieda

> "
> It is true that
> I am a trouble-
> maker, but not
> to the extent
> that I need to
> be expelled
> from class.

Diego Rivera is going to talk about Christianity in the arts!

[12] Isabel González Garduño.

9

15th September 1923

Dearly precious Mama

Today I was expelled from the maths class because Mr Palafox said that I was too much of a trouble-maker, and although they may tell you things about me, they are not true; that old man is very mean and it is true that I am a trouble-maker, but not to the extent that I need to be expelled from class. Toledano will send you a letter at noon with my father, but do not pay attention to anything he tells you, because they are a bunch of lies. I do in fact tell you when I am hanging out with the Cachuchas,[13] and we don't do bad things, but here at school they are alarmed about everything, and that gossip comes from Dolores Bolillo.

Today I will be at the amphitheatre with my classmates to attend Diego Rivera's talk. I did tell you about the first lecture and how much I liked listening to everything he said. Don't worry about me because I will walk to Zócalo with Carmen Jaime and take the train. Send my little red bag to the station with Aureliano, and if you'd like you can go with Cristina[14] and wait for me at Zócalo in Coyoacán. Bring my roller-skates so that we can stay at the square for a little while.

Good-bye and kisses
Frieda

[13] A political group Frida belonged to while at school at the Escuela Nacional Preparatoria. In 1927 she painted, *Si Adelita o Los Cachuchas* (*If Adelita or the Peaked Caps*).

[14] Cristina Kahlo, Frida's sister.

IO

18th May 1927

Dearly precious Mama

Don't worry about me, because I have been well. Maty already took me to see the Dr and tomorrow they will set my cast, here at Maty's house. I will tell you later how much it cost; you'll see if you can contribute with something, don't you think? Listen dear, let me know with Ricardo how you are doing, because I miss you very much. I also miss Papa; I think I will be leaving on Saturday because I feel embarrassed to make Paco[15] and Maty spend so much money.

Tell me how my bedroom is coming along, and how my little Caña is doing; say hello to everyone on my behalf: to Adri, Guero, little Carlos[16] and Kitty – (tell them to take good care of themselves). Tell me what you have told Grandma, regarding my whereabouts, because otherwise when I arrive I will be like the bear not knowing what to say.

Don't forget me and receive many kisses from your daughter
who loves you
Frieda

If it rains too much in Coyoacán and there is thunder, go to Adriana's house, because you know you get scared of thunder.

15
Francisco Hernández,
Maty's husband. His
nickname was 'Paco'.
16
Francisco Hernández's
son, Carlos Veraza Uthoff,
from his first marriage.

YOU ARE ALWAYS WITH ME

II

17th February 1930

Dearly precious Mama

Today I can't go home because I have to go with Diego to Cuernavaca to make arrangements for the bedroom where he is going to live while he paints over there. So we won't arrive until after dark. Tomorrow I will pay you back what you kindly lent me for the masons ($3.25), right? Please dear, beg the foreman to hurry up, because I want another mason to come in because it's $7.75 daily already and I don't know how I will get the money. When the new mason comes in, get him to start in the hall and the entry hall. I won't start painting the doors until tomorrow, because I haven't bought the paint.

Margarita[17] and Nicasia will clean the first two bedrooms. Watch them! I don't want them to stain the wall; you know, I want them to start washing them so that they take off the first layer of dirt. Don't you think?

Well dear, we'll see each other tomorrow.

Say hello to my Papa, to Kitty, to little Isolda,[18] etc.

And have a thousand kisses from your
little Frieda[19]

17
Margarita Kahlo, Frida's sister.

18
Isolda Pinedo Kahlo, Cristina Kahlo's daughter, Frida's niece – Frida refers to her as 'the girl' in letter 12 (p.41).

19
In Hispanic cultures, it is customary to use diminutives as terms of endearment. Frida Kahlo very often used the negative diminutive 'ucha' to create 'Frieducha' (little or scraggly Frieda), as is the case throughout her letters; but rather than her own coinage, 'Frieducha' is actually how her parents used to address her and it was used, in fact, as a term of endearment.

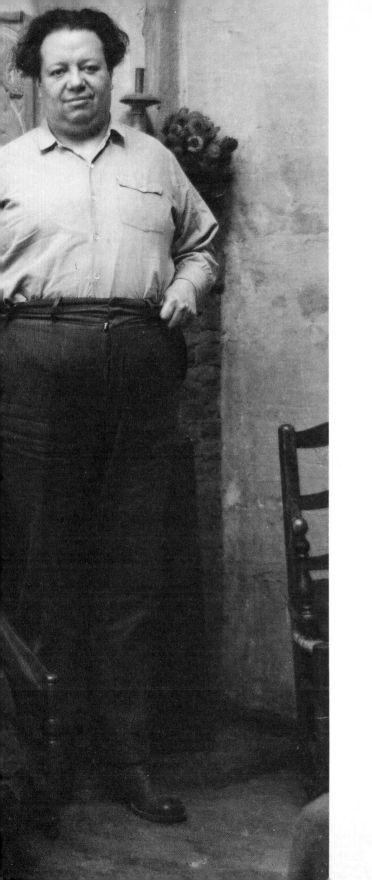

SAN FRANCISCO

AFTER FINISHING HIS MURAL AT THE PALACE OF CORTÉS IN CUERNAVACA, which was commissioned by the US ambassador to Mexico, Diego was asked to paint a mural at the Pacific Stock Exchange Luncheon Club in San Francisco. There he painted *Allegory of California* and, soon after, *The Making of a Fresco, Showing the Building of a City* at the San Francisco Art Institute.

Frida had never been abroad before; her impressions of the trip are vivid and she constantly compares what she sees and experiences in the US to Mexico. While in San Francisco Frida met Dr Leo Eloesser, a thoracic surgeon at Stanford University, who became one of her main doctors. Dr Eloesser provided ointment and frequent injections for her crushed right foot and the after-effects of her broken spinal column. He was to become a very close friend.

She depicts her relationship with Diego as loving and supportive; he seems to be generous in giving her money for her family. A constant theme in these letters is the financial support that Frida provides now that her father's commissions as a photographer have become scarce; Frida began to send her own money home and Diego paid off their mortgage.

ILLUSTRATION ON
PAGES 36–7
Frida and Diego in 1931,
soon after their marriage.

In these letters Frida expresses worries for her mother who is having problems with her gallbladder and a liver tumour; but also for her father, who suffered from epileptic seizures and later became deaf, although this is not explicitly mentioned in the letters.

Although Frida constantly complained about being bored while Diego was away working on his murals, San Francisco provided her with the independence and freedom to truly embrace the painter's craft and Diego suggested that she hold an exhibition there. While in San Francisco, she painted one of her most important and later award-winning paintings: *Frida and Diego Rivera* (1931) (p.110).

12

9th November 1930

Precious Mama

We finally arrived in San Francisco. In the next letter, I will tell you more in detail what I have seen; this letter is only for you to be at ease and to give you my address so that you all can write to me very often (the address is: Jessop Place 15, San Francisco, California). I want to know how everybody is doing, my father, Kitty, little Isolda, Mati, Adri; I mean, everybody. I think Diego's project will only take three or four months, and then we'll see each other again. We went to Los Angeles, it's beautiful; San Francisco is beautiful too, it's not cold at all and I feel very well so far. Please take very good care of Sombra[20] and the yellow cat.

Dear Mama, write to me right away because I want to know how you are doing, how your house projects are going and all the details about all of you. I will write to you daily. Tell Cristi that I will write to her too and to the chubby girls, and to my Papa. Say hello to Aunt Bela, to Caro, to Grandma, etc. I have not seen the Lunas yet, because I only got here today.

I will write to all of them, in the meantime say hello to them, as well as to Guero, to Carlos and to Paco; let me know how Uncle Pepe is doing.

20
Frida's favourite pet;
a female dog.

Diego says hello and sends lots of kisses to Kitty and to the girl. San Francisco is huge; with the Lunas I will dare to go out more often, but not alone because even locals get lost. The city is located in a marvellous place, the bay is gorgeous, and I was very impressed to see the ocean for the first time; on our journey we passed by the sea more than six times and the Pacific Ocean is amazing. Tell Kitty that I saw Dorotea in Los Angeles, she took me all over; we went to the beach which is exquisite, and the city is also huge. I went to Hollywood and visited the actors' and actresses' homes, which cost lots of money, and all the women here are scary and really obnoxious. I will write to you tomorrow with more time in hand, because everything here is done in a rush. Write to me.

Have a thousand kisses and all the love from your daughter
who adores you
Frieda

13

10th November 1930

Dearly precious Mama

Yesterday, when I arrived, I wrote you a very short letter that you ought
to have received already, but in this letter I will tell you more details all
about the trip and everything.

The train took seven and a half hours to depart, so in Guadalajara
we had to stay for a long time and I was able to see the whole city: the
museum, the churches, the most important things. We ate there and at
six-thirty we left for Nogales, Sonora. The trip along the way is
marvellous, because the train travels along the coast, Mazatlán, Tepic,
Culiacán, etc., until you reach Nogales, which is the border with the
United States; the blissful border is a wired fence that separates
Nogales, Sonora from Nogales, Arizona, but one can say that it's all the
same. At the border, the Mexicans speak English very well and the
gringos Spanish, but they both pretend they don't. At both sides of the
border they check your passports and they do a medical examination,
and then the train leaves for Los Angeles; one arrives more or less in
one full day and a night. I loved Los Angeles and so did Diego, it's a city
located in a wonderful place, and it has buildings which are very nice;
the beach is wonderful, but all the gringas are horrendous. The
actresses are not worth much. The millionaires live in Los Angeles and
poor people don't live well; imagine, a square metre of land in the city
centre costs five thousand dollars, that is to say, more than ten thousand
pesos. There are homes only for the very rich and for the film actors and
actresses, the rest are wooden homes and very poor looking. There are
three thousand Mexicans in Los Angeles who have to work like mules
to compete in business with the gringos. After Los Angeles you pass by
San José and San Bruno and then you arrive at San Francisco; it's an
enormous city; Diego says that it resembles London, because now we

> " Don't be sad,
> because I am
> doing very
> well, Diego is
> very kind to me
> and besides, I
> will heal better
> here than in
> Mexico.

YOU ARE ALWAYS WITH ME

have fog and the industrial neighbourhoods have all the aspect of the alleys in London (according to Diego).

Yesterday in the afternoon we were invited to a cocktail party at the house of the Director of the Stock Exchange,[21] which is where Diego is going to work. He has a wonderful house and from a little terrace you can see all of San Francisco and the bay and the lights of Berkeley, another city which is on the other side of the bay. The director speaks Spanish better than mine, and six or seven languages more. They have treated Diego very well, and they have liked me too. I am sending you here one of the newspapers in which we appear; we have appeared in something like six newspapers, but I have not been able to find them.

I am writing this with horrible handwriting, I am lying down because as usual I have some inflammation. But the wives of the other artists have treated me very well; one came over and put a hot-water bottle on me and another one swept the floors for me and cleaned the whole house. One is French and speaks Spanish, her name is Ginette,[22] and the other one is gringa, but they are both nice and good people.

We live in the sculptor's studio, Stackpole,[23] which has a Parisian style, a very large room like three times the living room of our house in Coyoacán. There is a drawing board, a chaise-longue, a sofa, a chimney and a desk; besides that, there is a small room which works like a dining room and a kitchen, with a big table. The boiler and the gas stove and the sink, for the cooking utensils, are very comfortable; then there is a bedroom with a bed where Diego can't sleep because it has a box spring that wobbles and a little chest of drawers to keep things and a Mexican chair, a warm showerhead and a toilet; all this is located on a rooftop, at Montgomery St. 716 or, by the other side, 15 Jessop Place. It's better that you write to me at the Montgomery address.

We just went out to have breakfast and dinner, but they are going to

21
Frida is talking about the Pacific Stock Exchange, where Diego painted *Allegory of California*.

22
Ginette Stackpole, Ralph Stackpole's wife.

23
Ralph Stackpole, (1885–1975). American sculptor, painter and muralist.

ask us to bring back milk, bread and butter, so that we then can go out and eat, and as I don't have to start a fire or anything, because everything is done with gas, it's not hard work for me.

We live very close to Chinatown, almost around the corner; Chinese men and women walk around like in a scene wearing their authentic costumes. So far I have only seen old Chinese women and children, who are beautiful; I haven't seen young Chinese women; they sell marvellous things, beautiful robes and lots of other things.

The ones who are really beautiful here are the boys; they are big and beautiful, but the girls are horrible and so are the men. (I will continue writing to you later because I am going to eat now).

Dear Mama, today I haven't gone out at all, as I told you, my inflammation is bad; most likely it was due to the long trip. Dr Eloesser[24] – who is the one that Diego wants me to see because of my spine – is going to come and see me at five-thirty and most likely tomorrow my inflammation will get better and then I will get frequent injections. The Dr is very nice, I met him yesterday, he speaks old Spanish very well and he is very intelligent. I will write to you later and let you know how I am doing with him.

I still haven't seen the Lunas because we have been so tired that I haven't felt like doing anything; I will probably look for them tomorrow.

I will tell you, little by little, all the details that I may forget. Just write to me and let me know about everything, how Papa is doing, if he's working and everything, because whatever money I am able to send you I will send it to you immediately. Also, tell me how Kitty and her beautiful daughter are doing, I want to know every detail of what they do. I will write to Mati and Adri in another letter, the same goes to Aunt Bela, little Caro, Grandma and everybody. Tell Papa that everything I tell you is as if I were telling him the same thing; tell him I send him many kisses, and

24
Leo Eloesser (1881–1976). An American doctor, who worked at Stanford University, when Frida Kahlo met him; and who became one of her main doctors throughout her life. Frida painted *Portrait of Dr Leo Eloesser* (1931) and dedicated one of her paintings to him, *Self-Portrait Dedicated to Dr Eloesser* (1940).

YOU ARE ALWAYS WITH ME

ask him not to be so stubborn and to remember to write to me. Say hello to Herminia and Chucho,[25] be very caring with Sombra as well as with Monroy; don't kick him out, because I would love to see him again; give the yellow cat more chicken skin than the rest.

Dear Mama, if Mr Magaña comes by, give him my address and ask Kitty to write in a letter whatever he may want to tell us, because he doesn't know how to write very well.

Write to me often; no one better than you knows the pleasure I get from receiving letters from all of you, especially yours. So don't stop writing to me. I will do the same daily, if I can. Send a thousand kisses to Papa, to Kitty, to her daughter and to everybody and for you all my love.

Your
little Frieda

Don't be sad, because I am doing very well, Diego is very kind to me and besides, I will heal better here than in Mexico

25
Chucho was one of the servants at the house, and later became one of Frida's assistants.

14

14th November 1930

Dear Mama

I am sending Papa a cheque for fifty pesos, if you want you can cash it, but I am sending it to him although I know that everything is for you, and I feel so sorry that he is not working and at least this money will encourage him a little, don't you think?

So far I haven't had a letter from any of you, but I hope that I will soon.

Lupe Luna came to see me at this very moment, she sends you lots of greetings, especially to Grandma and to Aunt Lupe and to Aunt Ana.

Tell Kitty not to forget sending me little Isolda's foot size, as well as hers and yours so that I can buy you Chinese sandals. Tell me if you need some money and I'll see if I can send it to you. I only have ninety pesos left at the Bank of Mexico, that's why I can't give you any of that money, but whatever money I get from Diego, I will send you what I can.

I send you a thousand kisses and all my love.
Your daughter
little Frieda

Postcard sent by Frida
from San Francisco,
around 1930

The Great Highway and Beach, San Francisco, Calif.   103

15

14th November 1930

Dearly precious Mama

I don't know if you got my other letters, I sent them airmail, but in case you didn't, you know I haven't forgotten you, not even for a moment, and although we are now so far away from each other, you are always with me everywhere I go. Send many greetings to my Papa, to Kitty and to her beautiful daughter. I am doing better than in the first few days because I am getting to know the city and the people much better, and above all, I am getting myself understood better; here I have to speak English by force; there is no other way. Diego hasn't started working yet and I am with him almost all day, but in a few days he will, and I will have to be alone, although the gringas that I have met are good people, I don't trust them too much; besides, I don't like friendships that much. I am going to paint, and Diego wants me to put on an exhibition here. This afternoon I will see the Lunas, I already spoke to them on the phone, but only the old man was there, and he doesn't remember me any more.

Tell Cristi that I miss her dearly, and that I am very sorry she didn't come; she would have been much happier, but let's see if next year she comes to New York with us.

Dear Mama, I want you to calmly explain to Papa, if it's possible for him to make copies of Tina's[26] negatives, they are at his office, on his board of negatives;[27] tell him to have them copied on Azo Paper nos. 1, 2, 3 and 4 as it's indicated in each negative; he can sell them for fifty cents each at Sonora News, with Mr Davis; Cristi can take them. Tell Kitty that especially the ones with the frescoes, they are separated and that way it is easier to know which one is which, the ones of the Secretary of Education and the ones of Chapingo. This should be of help to Papa, don't you think?

Have you already started working on your house project? I haven't had any letters from any of you, and I am dying to know how you all are doing. My address is Montgomery Street 716. San Francisco Cal. USA. Write to me as soon as you can because I miss you dearly.

I already saw Dr Eloesser and I am going to get better during all this time. I already wrote to Adri and Mati; tell Grandma and Aunt Bela that I will write to them very soon and that I send them lots of kisses, the same to Caro and Romerius; to Uncle Pepe and the girls, to Guera, etc. How is Sombra doing? How about the small cat and my parrot? Send many greetings to Herminia and Chucho. The following little letter is for Papa:

26
Tina Modotti (1896–1942). Italian photographer, model and political activist.
27
Frida's father, Guillermo Kahlo, was also a photographer.

Dearly precious Papa

I miss you dearly, you have no idea how much I would like to be with all of you, but I will soon be back and we'll see each other again. The city of San Francisco is very pretty, as well as the road we took to get here; I saw the ocean for the first time and I loved it; this city is located in a marvellous place, you can see the ocean from everywhere; the bay is huge and there are ships coming from China and the whole East. We live close to Chinatown; imagine, there are ten thousand Chinese here; they sell beautiful things in their shops, handmade costumes and fabrics, made out of very fine silk; when I return I will tell you more about it in detail.

I want you to write to me and tell me how you are doing, send me a message and I will be able to help you immediately. Diego says hello and sends you his regards; I don't want you to be so stubborn, it's bad for you, now that I am so far away from you, I beg you so, that way you and Mama will be happy all the time. If you don't have much work let me know and I will send you whatever you need, I am enclosing a cheque for $50.00 so that you can cash it at the Bank of Montreal, it's located at Isabel la Católica. Cristi will tell you how to cash it.

Send my greetings to little Isolda, and many kisses on my behalf.

Be caring with Sombra and the small dog, and give a million kisses to my dear Mama. Have all the love from your daughter who adores you.

little Frieda

OPPOSITE
Twenty-five-year-old
Frida, photographed by
her father.

21st November 1930

Dearly precious Mama

It was so nice to get your little letter as well as Papa's message. In Kitty's letter I learned that her daughter is doing better, but I had such a terrible anxiety because of that. Cristi also tells me that you are doing well but that my father is still getting upset, but now that I am not close to him I even miss his tantrums and everything; one doesn't know what one has until it is lost, that's why even though it may be hard on you, bear his tantrums and it's better not to pay attention to him. I had already written to you before getting your letter, so before you get this letter you'll know how I am doing. Regarding my spine and toe I feel very well; I haven't stopped getting any of my shots. The Lunas came to see me yesterday (Sunday), but they didn't find me because we went to eat at the woods in Santa Rosa, a beautiful place, you and Papa would have loved it; it has trees that are huge and older than a thousand years; it has a frozen lake and two theatres made with tree trunks, anyway, something delightful, we were happy and we arrived back in San Francisco at eleven at night.

"
Write to me whenever you can, because the day I get one of your letters is worth more than a party every day.

For the rest, every day is the same and nothing changes. Only my departure gets closer each day, and I am in a better mood. I am enclosing these pictures so that you more or less see what Burbank's[28] house looks like, that's where we ate last Sunday. Tell Papa to write to me in a little while, because I love his letters. Mati wrote to me and Paco sent a little message along; I'll reply to them today. Diego is doing well, his eyes are doing better and tell Kitty that he thanked her for her letter very much. How did you mend the railing in your house's hallway? Did you already pick up our writings? Please don't forget them. Send me a portrait of yours and one of Isolda; I want to see you even in portraits. Write to me whenever you can, because the day I get one of your letters is worth more than a party every day. Have a million kisses from your little daughter Frida[29] who adores you more each day and who doesn't forget you, not even for a moment.

little Frieda

28
Luther Burbank (1849–
1926). American botanist
and horticulturist. He
appears in Diego's mural,
Allegory of California.

29
Note that Frida wrote
'little Frida' and few lines
down, 'little Frieda'.

17

21st November 1930

Dearly precious Mama

You have no idea how happy I was to get your letter; I didn't know what else to do to know about all of you, and this morning when I was going to send you a telegram I found your letter in the letterbox and one previous letter from Kitty; likewise, I was very happy to get a letter from Papa, you know he doesn't write to anyone but he remembered me nonetheless. Now that I know how you all are doing, I am so very happy because I felt as if a train was going to run over me. Dear Mama, you shouldn't be sad for me because I am doing very well, I already started having injections since the beginning of this week and I feel very well; the only thing that hurts a little bit is my toe and as you know it has no cure, but other than that I have no pain and I am happy. The Dr says that I am going to feel much better with the injections and that there is no need to have an operation or anything, in case my toe wouldn't heal, he says that it would be better to have it cut because my nerves don't reach the tip of my toe and it would be constantly sick and an open wound. He prescribed an ointment to see if it gets better, otherwise I believe that the surgery on my toe is of no great importance, but it is not for sure yet. Regarding my spine and everything, he told me that I have the same that all doctors have said, which is hereditary, but with the injection treatment I will get a lot better so don't be sad at all because I am neither getting worse nor better, just the same as usual. And here I will get better than if I were in Mexico, because the doctor picks me up and drops me off at home each day I need to have the injections. In no way would I like you to be sad because I'll be upset with you. I think that by March we should be back in Mexico. I miss you dearly and my days become endless, and there is no other way but to be strong.

The gringas have liked me very much and they are impressed by the dresses and shawls that I brought with me, my jade necklaces are amazing for them and all the painters want me to pose for their portraits; they are naive, but very good people. They all have treated us very well. Stackpole, the sculptor, who is the owner of the studio where we live, is very nice and so is his wife; she speaks Spanish very well and we get along well; she mocks, like me, at all the presumptuous rich women from here; she is very humble and a good person.

I met a Mexican lady who is going to find a woman for me to do the house chores, that way I will have more time to go out and do whatever I want.

Diego has yet to start his painting on the wall, so all day long I go everywhere with him and we are happy, he's good to me and he loves me (so far) very much. We have attended several parties that the gringas have thrown in our honour, and let me tell you that you have no idea as to how dull these parties are; there are such scarecrows that would make the world tremble. So far, I haven't seen a beautiful woman, only in the Italian neighbourhood there are very beautiful ones, but a few, like everywhere in the world.

What I am fascinated about is the city; in whichever point you are, you will have a delightful view. A few days ago, at the pier, we boarded small boats that cross the bay, they are not that small, because they fit one hundred cars. We went to Fairfax which is more or less an hour and a half from here; it's beautiful and almost all the people who don't have any money live there, because in the city everything is very expensive.

The silk for the dresses, the stockings, the jumpers, everything is so expensive; and as we bring Mexican money, it costs double here, so it's a shame.

Tell me how little Isolda is doing, I miss her a lot; send me her portrait, tell Kitty not to forget it.

Send many greetings to Grandma, to Uncle Pepe and to Guera; anyway, to everybody. I got a letter from Carlos, which I will reply to.

Please send me Diego's correspondence. [Diego says hello!].[30]

How are Adri, Mati, Guero and Paco doing? Say hello to Herminia and Chucho, and be caring with my dogs and with my little yellow cat, and kiss the parrot.

In each letter I will tell you something of whatever I see over here; when you write to me, tell me how your house project is doing, how you are doing, everything that goes on; anyway, I want to know everything, detail by detail. Above all, don't be sad, because as I am telling you I am doing very well; only missing you terribly.

Have all my love and kisses from
your little Frieda

30
Note written on the side.

18

30th November 1930

Dearly precious Mama

Today in the morning I got your letter and one from Kitty, I was sad yesterday all day because I thought I was going to get letters from all of you but nothing came, but today in the morning about eleven I got them and I am delighted. I am very happy that all of you are doing well, and to get you very excited let me tell you that my toe is doing very well with the medication prescribed by the Dr and most certainly it won't be necessary to do anything else. So be happy regarding that; doctors speak too much and don't make much sense. I don't have news to tell you from here, because besides parties and meetings with old people, we haven't seen anything else. The other day we went to have dinner at a Chinese restaurant with the Chinese ambassador; he speaks French and English very well, he is very intelligent and nice, we had fun and two old gringos who were a little drunk made me laugh all night long; I was laughing so much with them, the party was amazing, but the rest of the people were dull and stupid. Yesterday (Sunday), we visited Stanford University, which is an hour and a half from here. It's like a big city; it has theatres, cinemas, swimming-pools, housing for professors and students; parks; anyway, it's an entire town. The university has ten thousand students, that way you can work out how big it is. In general, San Francisco and California as a whole, are very interesting; above all, San Francisco, because it has neighbourhoods with foreigners from everywhere in the world. In the

> Give the yellow cat more chicken skin than the rest ... How is Sombra doing? How about the small cat and my parrot?

Russian neighbourhood people are dressed like in Russia, and the girls dance in the hills; the Greek and the Japanese neighbourhoods are very interesting too, but especially the Chinese neighbourhood, because you can find everything there is in China; beautiful things. I would love to bring many things to all of you, but it's going to be impossible because it costs too much to get them across the border, so I'll bring whatever I can in my suitcases and that's it. I'll see if they'll allow me to ship something express post. I am happy to hear that your house project is progressing, because the only thing I want is for you to sort it out in the best possible way so that you are happy. How is Papa? As stubborn as usual? You can't imagine how much I miss him and how bad I feel that he can't see everything there is here, as he would have loved the bay, the boats, etc. Give him lots of kisses on my behalf. Tell me how little Isolda is doing, and if she has already started talking, tell me everything she is doing; I love her more each day and I believe that she must get prettier each day, right?

I thank you dearly for taking good care of all my pets; as you know, Diego loves them very much. Does Sombra take to the streets as much?

How is my Uncle Pepe doing? And my Grandma? If you see Rouaix say hello to him and tell him that I am going to write to him. Say hello to my Aunt Bela, to Romero, to Caro, and to everybody. Maty wrote to me, so did Adri, so that's why I am not asking you about them.

Have you already started the work on your kitchen and bathroom floors? Tell me if the money I sent you was enough and if you already bought the motor, which is absolutely necessary. On Wednesday, I will probably go to Los Angeles by plane with Diego and Dr Eloesser; I will tell you how I felt, if I vomited or not, and believe that I will most certainly get dizzy, but I am eager to board the plane. It's only three hours from here to Los Angeles. It isn't confirmed yet, but I think we will travel. Diego sends you many greetings, the same to Kitty and the girl, and Papa. Say hello to Herminia, and write to me as soon as you get my letter, because you can't imagine the pleasure I get to read your letters and to hear about you. Send many kisses to Papa, to Kitty and to little Isolda. What happened with Cristi's divorce?

The lawyers are a bunch of donkeys, don't you think? Your letter should get here soon, in the meantime I am sending you in this letter all my love, and thousands of kisses from your girl.

little Frieda (I will soon send you pictures of us)

19

Fairfax, California
4th December 1930

Dearly precious Mama

I am writing to you now from a little town close to San Francisco, that is called Fairfax. I am at Ginette Stackpole's house because Diego went to a town that's even farther away, to draw some mines. And since I was going to get tired of walking, I decided to stay with Stackpole's wife; she is very good to me. I have been here since yesterday and I will stay until Sunday, that's when Dr Eloesser will come to get me and then we'll meet Diego in Sacramento (that's where Diego went, which is California's capital). So I don't know if in these last three days I have had letters from you or not, but I hope to find one on Monday. I want you to write to me more often, because as the days go by I miss you more and more. Diego's project is taking long because this month we have attended a lot of stupid parties, and they have barely let him work. He hasn't started working on the fresco yet, so I don't know when we will return to Mexico; now I am thinking that if Kitty had come along she would have been terribly bored, because after the novelty is over, it's the same everywhere.

I am painting because they want me to do an exhibition before we leave. It's an opportunity because I can sell some and help you out more, and it would be more than foolish on my part if I miss this chance, don't you think? Maybe we'll move to a hotel so that I have time to paint during the whole day, and I wouldn't have to worry about sweeping the floor and nonsense like that; in the meantime you can all keep writing to me at the same address. It was such a pleasure to get a letter from Grandma, she always remembers me. Tell me how she and my uncle Pepe are doing, I'm always afflicted, because I feel so sorry for them.

In my last letter to Cristi I sent a cheque to pay for the remainder at Cuernavaca ($60.00 dollars); the cheque number is 9774, at it's from Diego's account in dollars at the Bank of Montreal; in a letter for you, I am also sending you a cheque, number 60270, for twenty pesos, from my silver account;[31] I am telling you all these details because in case the letters get lost and don't reach you in time, alert the bank immediately, and tell them not to pay these cheques, because the letters got lost.

How's Papa doing? Is he working? I hope I can sell some paintings so that I send you money, because my greatest fear is that you won't have enough money, and I never hear about it. Diego's birthday is on 13th September; if you can, it would be good if you send a telegram congratulating him, but if it's too costly just a letter although it may arrive later, but those things are not that important to him.

Cristi told me that Paco was upset. What happened? Write to me a lot and with full details, you have no idea what your letters mean to me. How are the girl and Kitty doing? Maty has not replied to my last letter. Carlos wrote to me and I am expecting another letter from Adri, Aunt Bela and Caro.

I am already doing a lot better. My toe has completely healed. I always wrap it around with cotton, so that it doesn't touch my shoe. What happened to Mrs Lola? Did she fail to go with Aunt Lupe? Tell me in detail about what's new, and above all, about how you are doing; how your house project is going; everything.

31
Silver peso account.

So far I don't have any news, because we do much the same thing every day; we eat breakfast at the studio, Diego starts working and I do the same; at twelve we eat at the Italian restaurant (the gringos eat very early here); then we come back to the studio, and we have dinner at seven. Sometimes we go out at night to get to know the city a little more, or attend parties organised by other painters. The day before yesterday they cooked a Mexican dinner for us; they arranged several tables, like in the restaurants, with the Mexican flag. They cooked us stuffed tortilla, tamales and beans; the stuffed tortillas were good, but not hot at all; the tamales were not any good, but the beans were delicious. I ate too much beans, because I had not even smelled them for a month. It was nice they made the effort, because they eat too differently (and horribly); but, anyway, I am sort of getting used to their food, and since I get very hungry due to the injections, I eat whatever they give me. In the mornings I drink two glasses of milk and cream and two oranges; bread and butter, etc. (which I never did before, but it's much better, let's see if my skinny and bony appearance goes away).

Dear Mama, don't forget to write to me extensively and to kiss and to say hello to Papa, to Kitty and the girl (she must be so sweet, right?); in general, to everybody, to Herminia and Chucho too, and to the family of dogs, cats and parrots. Don't be sad because of me, pray to God that these months pass by quickly so that I see you again and kiss you lots. In the meantime, even though in a letter, I send you all my love and a million kisses.

Your little Frieda

Has Carmen Jaime come round? (If she does, say hello to her).

YOU ARE ALWAYS WITH ME

20

San Francisco, California
8th December 1930

Dearly precious Mama

It's been many days since I last got one of your letters. Why don't you write to me more often? I am always so anxious to know about how you are doing; the same with Papa, the girl and Kitty.

In terms of health I am doing well. I have a good appetite and I eat a lot; I continue getting the injections. I am writing this letter to let you know that yesterday (Sunday), I got on a plane; I went with Dr Eloesser to Sacramento. I loved the trip and you can't imagine how beautiful it is; it's very comfortable and you don't feel anything bad; on the contrary, we travelled with the mail plane which was wonderful. It took us one hour and a half from Oakland to Sacramento, and we got back at night to see Diego and Ralph, who already were at the mines. Diego did beautiful drawings of the mines and the miners; there are some very interesting fellows, and generally speaking, the city of Sacramento is very interesting. There are weird people. Diego sends you lots of greetings; he's now drawing and I am writing from a huge chair that we have close to the fireplace. Here in San Francisco it hasn't been too cold, only a little bit at night, but during the day I can go out wearing percale dresses. It's now eleven at night and I am already going to go to sleep; I believe I will get letters from you tomorrow. The first thing I do in the mornings is to check the postbox to see if there is a letter, and when there is none, I am upset all day.

I am already painting and that way I am less bored, because otherwise my boredom would be horrible.

Does my Papa have work? Tell me with confidence. Tomorrow I'll send you fifteen or twenty dollars by telegraph. If you get a telegraph message, you have to cash in at their office. Obviously, the message will arrive before this letter, but I tell you this for a future occasion. Don't forget that the date to collect the promissory note from Carlos Mérida[32] (31st December) is approaching. How's the girl doing? I often get letters from Kitty and I know through her how you and everybody are doing; she is a very good person with me. Adri and Mati have also written to me, and so has Caro.

How is my Uncle Pepe doing? And Grandma? Say hello to Herminia, Chucho and the whole doggy and animal family in general.

The Dr finds me much better, so take it easy and write to me. Each day that passes by is one day less to return, and for that I am happy. I never forget you and you have no idea how much I miss you. Diego even makes fun of me because he says I am like a little girl. Well dear, take very good care of you and have all the love of

your little Frieda

32
Carlos Mérida (1891–1985).
Guatemalan artist, who
was also involved in the
Mexican muralist
movement.

Postcard sent by Frida
from San Francisco,
around 1930

Cliff House and Seal Rocks, San Francisco, California   84

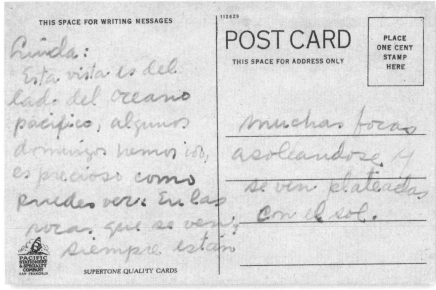

THIS SPACE FOR WRITING MESSAGES

Linda:
Esta vista es del
lado del oceano
pacífico, algunos
domingos vamos ió,
es precioso como
puedes ver. En las
rocas que se ven,
siempre están

POST CARD

THIS SPACE FOR ADDRESS ONLY

PLACE
ONE CENT
STAMP
HERE

muchas focas
asoleandose, y
se ven plateadas
con el sol.

SUPERTONE QUALITY CARDS

21

11th December 1930

Dearly precious Mama

It's been three days since I last got letters from any of you; tomorrow I most certainly will, but these days I have been terribly uneasy because of all of you, and with a devilish mood. Don't be bad and write to me more often; when I receive a letter from you my mood and everything changes and I get very happy. Kitty writes to me more often, but you at least have to write to me twice a week, do you want to? Yesterday Diego delivered a lecture at the 'Legión de Honor' Palace; a lot of people went and they all congratulated him, he is the big deal here in San Francisco. Poor him, they didn't even let him go to the toilet, they pester him all day.

(If you see Magaña say hello to her.)

I am doing well, I continue getting the injections and I don't feel as tired any more; the only thing is that I sometimes get really bored and I feel like coming back to Mexico, even riding on a donkey. I haven't been able to send you money this week, because Diego has only given me the basics, but I'll see if I will be able to send you some next week. You can't imagine how much I would like to give you all you need, so that you can finish your house project and everything, but now I am short of money and I can't. However, I am hopeful that I will be sending you money, little by little.

It's great to hear that your house project is advancing very well, and once it's done if you want to move some of your things, I think you will need to find someone to stay and take care of the house, don't you think? I think we'll stay here, more or less, for three months because Diego will start painting in a few days. How are Papa, Kitty and little Isolda doing?

Please tell Kitty that I sent her daughter a little present, and tell her to let me know if she got it. Dear Mama, write to me often because I miss you very much and I want to know everything that goes on – everything – because I am always uneasy because of you. Did you get ill?

(Say hello to Herminia and Chucho.)

Tell me everything you do and everything that happens to you, that way I'll be happier here.

Diego sends you lots of greetings, the same to Kitty and her daughter. I have nothing new to tell you so far, I am waiting for your letters in order to reply to all of you immediately.

Say hello to everybody. How is Uncle Pepe doing?

(Send kisses to Papa.)

How's Grandma? I send you kisses and all my love. (I will send you the newspaper clippings in which we have appeared, please put them in a very safe place for me.)

Your girl who adores you and never forgets you
little Frieda

22

18th December 1930

Dearly precious Mama

You have no idea how sorry I am regarding your issues with the damned masons, you must have got really angry, but Cristi told me that they mended the cracks again, right? I am expecting one of your letters any day now, because in several days I haven't got anything, just one from Kitty and one from Adri and I replied to them both already; Mati also wrote to me and she must have had my reply already. How have you been, Mama? You have no idea how much I miss you, and I don't stop thinking of you, not even for a moment. I am painting and that way I get some distraction, because otherwise I would be terribly bored. Is Papa working? What is he doing? How is he doing? Is he still as stubborn? I just got back from seeing the doctor, to get my injection, I have felt a lot better and I am in the mood to do things, to paint, etc., because the first days I was very sad. Last night we went to see a puppet theatre company, it was marvellous, you would have liked it, because the puppets were very well done, and they moved them around very well; they are really clever, and you know that I have always liked puppets. Diego is working hard to start on his project soon, and I hope we won't be here more than three months. They took magnificent pictures of me, I'll send you copies as soon as I get them. I sent the girl clothes, which will get there on 3rd January, when she turns two; she must be gorgeous. The days of my return, before I see you and everyone else, turn endless and you can't imagine how much so. Kitty has not mentioned anything regarding how her divorce is going, and what happened to Pinedo. You tell me how that issue is going. Rosita Rouaix's sister came to see me, she is a scary old lady like Xavier, her brother, and very silly.

I am going to ask you, if you can, to send me by post a can or jar of chilli pepper in vinegar, because with the food over here I am already cross-eyed, and I'd like something hot; I can find tortillas here, but although they look like donkey hide, they are not that bad. Is Paco still giving you something? I get desperate for not being able to send you what you need, but as I have to ask Diego for each [...].[33]

33
The rest of the letter is missing.

23

25th December 1930

Dearly precious Mama

Today, on Christmas day, I am writing to tell you what I did. We went to the house of some Italian people, the Piazonis, and we had a good time. The streets and the homes in San Francisco are full of Christmas trees that are lit, and it looks great, everybody sings and all the families get together for dinner; and they wait until midnight. You probably didn't go anywhere, but I don't know if my sisters threw a little party; anyway, tell me what you have done for the nine-day pre-Christmas celebration, and above all, if the girl is doing better already. I am always worried about all of you, and I am sure one of you is ill and you don't tell me anything about it. Has Papa had any work? You can't imagine how desperate I get for not knowing if you need anything and me not being able to help in any way; there are days in which I only think about that and I wish I could go back, but I beg you, that if you need money, because Papa is not working or anything, to please let me know; I'll see what I can do to send you money. These days I haven't been able to ask Diego for money, because he has spent too much, but in a few days it's possible that I may have some and I'll send it to you straight away; tell Kitty that in my last letter I was telling her that I was sending her money, but I forgot to include it in the letter, and I dropped it in the post, but in my next letter I will send her what I promised. Tell me how you are doing, how you feel, if Papa is okay; the girl, Kitty, everybody. There are times when you can't imagine how much I miss you, and I go crazy thinking that I still have several months before I go back, but on the other hand, I think this is the only chance I have to know something new, and for other people to get to know me, which will help me, later on, to sell my paintings, don't you think?

I am painting a lot, almost every day; it's the only way time goes by and I am able to put my mind off things, and not be too sad. Don't ever forget

> " Post a can or jar of chilli pepper in vinegar, because with the food over here I am already cross-eyed, and I'd like something hot.

YOU ARE ALWAYS WITH ME

Mérida's promissory note. Tell Kitty to send me Carlos Mérida's address, so that I send him a letter in case he didn't pay or in case something happens.

You can't imagine, I am doing much better in terms of health, and can easily do things and without getting tired, and I am in a better mood; the thing is that here I am actually getting better constantly; in Mexico I never did. Say hello to Coronado in case you see him, and to Landa, Rouaix and the Canets.

How's Uncle Pepe doing? You can't imagine how sorry I feel for him. Is Grandma doing okay? Tell Aunt Bela and Caro that they are very ungrateful; I wrote to them and they haven't replied at all.

Here are two proofs of pictures of me, I don't have copies yet; don't place them close to the sun because they'll turn black. They took pictures of me from many angles, but I am sending you the best ones.

If at night, when people are not bothering you, you have some time, write to me at least a few paragraphs, because I miss you dearly and you have no idea what a pleasure I get from your letters. Tell Papa that I send him many kisses, the same to Kitty and the girl; and that he should write to me, even a little bit, in your same letter.

Diego is doing well; he is working a lot, and he sends you many greetings and kisses to little Isolda.

Tomorrow I'll be going to Sacramento and I will come back the day after tomorrow; I hope to have the joy of finding letters from any of you, in the meantime, I am sending you, as usual, all my love and a million kisses.

Your daughter who adores you
little Frieda

24

30th December 1930

Dearly precious Mama

Today, in the morning, I received your little letter, Papa's photo and the notecards from the girl and Herminia. You can't imagine the pleasure I got, because I was not expecting anything. I was very upset the days before, and poor Diego didn't know what else to do with me, because all day I was making faces, but today, as whenever I get one of your letters, I have been very happy!!

In terms of health, I am doing well, just with a little cold and a headache, but this is not a big issue. I am very happy to learn that you and everybody else are doing well. You have no idea how much I thanked Papa for being so sweet and having sent me the photograph (although I know very well that it must have been your idea). Diego is very grateful and there is a little message from him in the letter I sent Papa. With regards to Uncle Pepe, I am very sorry, because it's very difficult that he will survive, don't you think? But, on the one hand, he will be relieved of so much suffering. I haven't done anything new, that's why I don't have much to tell you; I paint and go out a little every day.

I am surprised Kitty tells me she has not got her daughter's present yet, because I sent it many days ago; hopefully she'll get it one of these days. How is your house project going? Carmen Jaime wrote to me; I got her letter yesterday, poor her, she never forgot me.

Diego finished the drawing for the fresco already, and he'll soon start painting. I spoke on the phone with the Lunas and they send you many greetings.

Dear Mama, please let me know how much the paint for the doors would cost me, and I'll send you money. Did you already get the money from Carlos Mérida? Tell me what's going on about it; I'll see what we can do in case that bastard doesn't pay. Do you go to the cinema on Sundays? I almost always go out on Sundays; I have only been to the cinema here once, not even once to the theatre, and during the week my life is very monotonous. I just wait for your letters because that, and having Diego, is the only thing I care about.

I can't write any more because as I am telling you, I have nothing new to say, but if I were only to send you two lines, in them I would send you the love, and a thousand kisses, from the girl who adores you, and greatly misses you.

Your
little Frieda

25

1st January 1931
Happy new year!!

Dearly precious Mama

Today, 1st January, I am writing this letter to let you know how we awaited the new year. (Yesterday I replied to your previous letter.) Here in San Francisco, during 'new year', everybody gets really drunk despite the 'ban', that's the main and most important thing; other than that, they are like any person who is drunk but (not as crazy as to eat fire[34]). They take to the streets and sing and dance and they all shout at each other from the other side of the pavements, 'Happy new year!!'

    We went to eat at a *German* restaurant with Dr Eloesser, he likes everything German style; he plays the violin, he sings; oh, he dances too! And he drinks beer, and he always discusses about philosophy ... (in some ways he resembles, like two drops of water, my father). After having dinner, we went to the Dr's house to drink fruit punch, and to sing – with a guitar and a violin – Mexican, American, Russian, French, etc., songs; and everything was going well until the moment the Dr pulled out an aged and almond-tasting Tequila bottle, from Mexico, and put it on the table. Then the party really started and Diego drank so much that he started telling all the generals and government officials from Mexico to go to hell; he started speaking in French about European painting and finally he danced none other than huapango! We were there until three in the morning, and then we went to the Embarcadero with Clifford Wight[35] and his wife, who were with us; then things started there, because Diego insisted on sailing to Berkeley, at that time, saying that he was from Guanajuato proper and that he would go to Berkeley by force; after so much effort that it took us to convince him, we came back home and when coming in (Clifford and his wife had left for their home), how surprised would I be! Right there at the door, there was a man lying, as if dead; he was a young fellow, maybe twenty-two years old. After seeing

34
Mexican expression. A person can be drunk, but would never dare to hurt him/herself with fire.

35
Diego's assistant while in the United States.

YOU ARE ALWAYS WITH ME

him, Diego was shaken up a little, and he grabbed one of those milk bottles, and as much as I spoke to this fellow he wouldn't answer nor did he seem to be breathing. I thought he was being just a fool, and that maybe he would carry a gun, so in a good voice I yelled in English at him and asked him what he wanted, I asked him to leave and he wouldn't answer anything; I was so scared I thought I was going to die, but in the middle of all that horrible scene, because the door's light bulb is red and the man looked like a cadaver, Diego, instead of telling him something in English, he started saying, 'Mister, zócalo merced, Mister, Zócalo! o lo mando a la puritita . . . yo soy de puro Guanajuato! Mister!!' ('Mister, zócalo merced, Mister, Zócalo! or I'll send you to . . . I am from Guanajuato proper! Mister!!').[36] Well, let me tell you, my fear went away then and I started laughing, then after a while the man woke up, and the first thing he did was to laugh, but he was really boisterous, as I had never heard in my life. And he would turn his eyes white in a horrible way, and Diego and I had a bottle in hand; we were just waiting for him to attack us, so we would smash his head. He was probably drunk, not with alcohol but with cocaine or something like that, because he was sort of blue and his lips were shaking; he was handsome and he had blonde hair, but in that state, the bastard looked like a nightmare! Finally, very carefully, he begged me to leave him there, otherwise, he said they would take him (the police, I think), and that he didn't carry a gun with him, or any other weapon. In this country, I even distrust my own shadow, and I asked Diego to take him out to the streets, and the man would keep on falling in a way that would get to me; because it was weird, as if he were crazy. Diego, at the Montgomery Street exit door, kicked him in the ass and the man left; but he scared us (me in particular, because Diego barely noticed) in such a way that I felt that I was going to wake up . . . with trips to the bathroom.

36
'Zócalo' is the main square in Mexico City, and 'merced' ('La Merced') is a neighborhood close to Zócalo.

Afterwards, Diego fell asleep on a chair with the bottle in his hand and I fell asleep, and I woke up today at twelve and just now, poor Diego took off his clothes and went to bed.

That's how we spent 'new year'.

I hope, dear, that you all had a better time, and please tell Papa, Kitty and little Isolda (who will turn two the day after tomorrow) that I wish them a really, really good year, and for you, with all the love that you know your little Frieda has for you, I wish you many years of great joy, and hopefully I will soon be there so that we spend time together.

A thousand kisses from your little Frieda

26

13th January 1931

Dear precious Mama

I learned through Kitty that you and Papa are doing well, but in terms of money I am very concerned, because I perfectly know that poor Papa can't physically work like he used to, besides, the situation is really bad everywhere. That's why I tell Cristi that it would be hard for her to find a job and that, in the meantime, I will definitely send you something each month and along with what Paco provides, you will more or less make it; I wouldn't want you to rent your house before you live in it first.

Mama, tell me how your health is doing, the same with Papa and the little girl. I am doing well, I paint all day and I almost don't go out; I don't have much fun because at night San Francisco is a dead city.

About a week ago, there was a dinner party at a Mexican restaurant, for a painter who left for Europe; I ate Mole sauce, tortillas and stuffed tortillas and I sang corridos, 'la Cucaracha', 'Adelita' and a number of other songs, and all the gringos liked me; the dinner was nice, I went with my embroidered shirt and rebozo shawl and I was the centrepiece; because here they are too dull and any silly thing catches their attention; however, we had a lot of fun. The Dr who is treating me gave me a beautiful guitar and I already know how to play it; I sometimes spend the afternoons with Diego singing Mexican songs and always remembering you. Papa wrote to me, I'll reply today. Unfortunately, the return to Mexico will take a while and my eyes are already turning because of this. I am always sad because of you and I will never be able to get used to not being with you; the gringas here are like donkeys, they don't give a damn about anything; the same thing regarding their parents or children and they live like dogs; but we are not the same, and I suffer a lot for being far away from all of you, and without being able to hear from you, regarding what goes on with everybody, but through letters.

Dear Mama, if you can, write to me, as little as it may be, okay?

Diego says hello to you and to everybody. Don't let Carlos Mérida sleep, that way at least you'll have some money these days as Papa is out of work.

Otherwise, everything is the same, Diego works all day with the drawings and we'll soon start to paint; hopefully we'll at least be there at the end of March.

Say hello to Grandma, to Aunt Bela, to Lupe and Ana, and Caro and above all to Papa and to my beautiful and little Isolda, who must be more beautiful each day, and you precious Mama, have the love from your

little Frieda who adores you

The enclosed letter is to see if Kitty is able to find a job with this old man.

27

15th January 1931[37]

Dearly precious Mama of my life

Your little letter arrived today in the morning, before waking up; last night we went to bed at four in the morning because we went to a play and afterwards to a place where African-Americans do a competition of endurance. Imagine, they had been walking for two months without stopping; sixteen African-American couples (a man and a woman) started off and yesterday was the last night; only two remained. They started off walking at midnight without resting for a second, after two months of walking and walking, resting only for five minutes every hour, along a stretch of ten square metres, they endured the first hour very well, not so much the second hour and so on and so forth until two of them fell to the ground, exhausted, and the other ones won one thousand dollars each. Imagine that the ones who won were women and the men were not able to endure any longer, you have no idea how interesting this spectacle was, but the most cruel and stupid; they chain the black people, a woman and a man; there was a woman with a kid in her arms; two died and an unfortunate woman became mad from walking and her husband, instead of exiting the rink, picked up another woman and kept on walking; at the end, the ones who won, who were a twenty-three-year-old and a thirty-year-old, walked 1,680 hours! What a horrible thing!! We left from there at almost five in the morning. While those at the competition walk, some black women dance, marvellous, and others sing; there must constantly be noise because otherwise, the ones at the competition would fall asleep immediately, but as I say, it's incredibly cruel, as the misery those poor people are in forces them to do those horrible things. Imagine walking for two months!

37
Frida writes 1930, but the year is in fact 1931.

Precious Mama, you have no idea how happy I am to learn that you are doing well, as are Kitty, Papa and the girl, and that she liked the little toys I sent. I would like to send her wonderful gifts but I can't, because Diego hasn't been paid yet, and I can't be asking him for money now, so I'll send her other things later on as well as the money I promised you in my previous letter.

Regarding the paint for the doors, windows, etc., I don't think $30.00 is expensive, but I think that for now it's best to leave it as it is, because it will take us still some time before we get there, and it's best that a little before we leave he starts painting; he should put off the hall until I get there, because you know that Diego is a little odd when it comes to choosing colours and it's better he tells me how to choose them, but I want the entry hall and the doors in green, as they originally were, because that's the colour that looks best; so please tell the man to come back in a month or month in a half, so that he starts then and in the meantime I'll send you the thirty pesos and extra for the paint.

For now, I don't have a great deal to tell you because there is no news. I am really doing better, because, as you know, in Mexico I wasn't getting better at all. One of these days, I'll send you something that I think you will like. Also, Adri says that little Isolda appeared again in the Esperanza cinema as a little angel; I would have given away anything to see her, she must have looked beautiful, right? You can't imagine how much I thanked poor Kitty for the pilgrims and for all the little things she sent me; Diego was delighted, eating away quince cheese and peanuts.

> " Diego drank so much, that he started telling all the generals and government officials from Mexico to go to hell.

Tell Papa that I send him a thousand kisses and not to stop doing what I suggested to him (not to be so stubborn) and to behave well.

Say hello to Grandma, to poor Uncle Pepe, to Guera and the girls, etc., etc., and you my dear, have the entire heart of your

little Frieda

(If you can, write to me soon). Say hello to Mati, Paco, Guero, Chula and Carlos.

28

24th January 1931

Dearly precious Mama

I am very worried because Kitty told me that she already has a job (although without pay) at the university, and I imagine you will stay at home with little Isolda all day, try to always have Herminia keeping an eye on you, or at least Carlos, the idiot, because I am scared that, being all by yourself, something could happen to you or that you would need something without having anybody around. Don't let Chucho leave the girl alone, that way you would be able to do something, as the girl is at a terrible age. Today I got a letter from Kitty, from Papa, from Aunt Bela and from Carlos Veraza; so I heard from everybody that you are relatively well, and that, at least, makes me a little happy. Cristi tells me that Mérida has not paid the rest, and I think it would be good if you keep on bothering him so that he doesn't ignore you, because you need that money more than he does and also, why did he promise to repay that money if he wasn't going to able to, don't you think? So, tell him that from that money, you have to pay the workers or something like that, and that Diego doesn't know he hasn't paid, that way he'll see what he's doing and he will pay some.

So far, I am doing well Mama, so don't worry about me. The Dr with whom I am getting cured is a very good person and he doesn't skip any of my two weekly injections; when I feel lazy I don't go, he would then call me, very upset, the next day, so I will have to get cured either way. I eat a lot better and I drink a lot of milk, so I hope I feel better, because that would be a huge advantage, don't you think? Diego already started painting three days ago, poor him, he comes back exhausted at night, because that kind of work is for mules, not people; imagine, yesterday he started at eight-thirty in the morning and came back today at nine in the morning, more than twenty-four hours of work, nonstop; he didn't eat or anything, he was exhausted. He is good to me, I am the one who gets the Frida side in her head, and gets upset many times, but he is of good character and at least he seems to love me, I also love him a lot.

I am painting and I hope I get to do the exhibition (?). Life sometimes is interesting here, because there is lots to see; people are just everywhere, talkative and gossipy, etc., etc., but as they leave you alone I can easily work and live well. Yesterday, Diego delivered a lecture at an old ladies' club; they were like four hundred scarecrows, they were all about two hundred years old, tying their necks, because otherwise they would hang in the shape of waves; anyway, horrible old ladies, but very kind, they came to see me as if I were a weird animal, because I was the only young one and two or three more of us nearly over thirty, so they really liked me, but they would suffocate me by talking so much to me; the worst part, they spit when they talk, like Mr Campos, and they all have dentures, that move in all directions; well, let me tell you, there were such old iguanas that would stop the hiccups on anybody and they beat Carmen Jaime, in terms of beauty!

Some nights we watch scenes by Chaplin or other actors, at a sculptor's studio, who is very nice.

Dear precious Mama, please tell me how to make crêpes (don't forget, please?). I wrote to Grandma but she hasn't replied yet. How's poor Uncle Pepe doing? Tell him that I'll write to him this week. (Say hello to everybody).

You, dear, take very good care of yourself; don't pretend to be courageous and go up and down by yourself as something can happen to you, God forbid, because I am terribly worried because of you; don't be bad and pay attention to me, okay! Don't go by yourself anywhere.

I hope Cristi can find something more permanent. Kiss the girl lots, and tell Papa that today I will write him a letter in reply to his, which I loved! Send kisses to Kitty too. Say hello to Herminia and tell her to write to me, and not to cold shoulder me. And you, dear, have as usual, the love and the heart of

your little Frieda who adores you

29

30th January 1931

Dearly precious Mama

It's been almost eight days since Kitty wrote to me last. Today I got a letter from Mati and she tells me you are doing well, but I would like Cristi to write to me more often, because that's the only way I know how you are doing; otherwise, I am always afflicted because of you.

Adri is the one who tells me everything with more details, she says that they are already taking care of your house, is that right? You had not told me that they had stolen the pipe from your bathroom. How did it happen?

Yesterday I went to see the Lunas, they were pleased and they send you lots of greetings. I am sorry that poor Uncle Pepe is still not doing well. By chance, Isabel Magaña was there too, I didn't remember her face any more, and I found her really ugly and really obnoxious; too romantic and sentimental; was she always like that? She remembers Mati and Carmela a lot, as well as everybody in general. Rodolfo's daughter is horrible, she looks like a full moon but with glasses and a really big snout, and above all, really unintelligent. Tell my aunts not to write to them any more at the Pine 930 address, because they moved today to Broadway 1666.

Dear Mama, please tell me how you have been, if anybody is ill or anything like that; anyway, I would like to know what you are doing every five minutes, but it's impossible, but it would be enough for me if Cristi writes to me. How is it going with her at the university? Has Carlos Mérida still not paid you? Because I hope he does soon, because you need that money urgently for the motor and the installation. Diego is already progressing a lot, but I don't think he'll finish before March, so imagine how I feel when I think about having three more months before I see you. Has Papa found a job? How is he doing? Ask him to write to me whenever he can. I sent you some money the day before yesterday; tell me if you got it because, God forbid, the letter got lost. What do you think about poor Mrs Hernilda, I felt very sorry. Dear Mama, and what do you do with little Isolda all day? She must terrorise you. Adri says that she already says many words, tell me which ones. Now I am left alone every day and I am painting all the time, because otherwise I would die of boredom and sadness; I go out very little. The Dr already saw Diego and he says that what he has is kidney-related, but without consequence; poor him, he is literally exhausted at night and he only sleeps four or five hours. I am doing very well, I eat much better, but I am always missing you dearly and I can't ever be happy without all of you. Tell Papa that I send him lots of kisses and the same to Kitty and the girl.

Dear Mama, I also want to know how much I owe for the telephone bill, the motor, the instalments, etc., because I only left you money for three months and they are over; ask Kitty to send me a list, exactly with what is needed, so that I'll send you money for three more months because I don't know how much exactly it would be, given the food of so many pets and everything. Don't forget, dear, because you shouldn't be spending money on pet food, dogs, cats, parrots, rabbits, and on the many things that are needed. I would love to send you all that you need, but what can we do about it, there is no way. I won't ask you to write to me too much, because I understand you must be exhausted at night and the girl doesn't let you do anything during the day, but on Sundays, when Cristi is at home, try to write to me, at least a little bit, because you can't imagine the pleasure I get from receiving your letters. I don't have anything new to tell you, because as I tell you, I go out very little, besides, I already know most of San Francisco, and there are things that are hard to explain in a letter; when I come back I'll let you know in detail.

Ask Kitty to tell me what happened to Chicho Bassolo, but in full detail. And Paco, the saint, what did they do? Did they go to Mati's house? Have you seen Alfonso Rouaix? How's his arm doing? Poor Grandma, she wrote to me and tells me she's very afflicted because of Uncle Pepe; I feel so sorry. Aunt Bela also wrote to me.

Say hello to the postman, to Herminia and to Chucho. If I didn't miss you as much as I do, I would be happier here, because people have been very nice to us, and Diego is happy he is painting here, because he has a lot of instruments for his drawings, etc., because you know, he loves machines, factories and all that. But I can't get used to living far away from you, from Papa, from Cristi and little Isolda, and I think of all of you the whole day.

However, I am happy as I am learning something new and I have come across beautiful things. I hope time flies so that I am back in Mexico to see you again, and to tell you all that I have seen and liked here; in the meantime, take very good care of yourself, and don't worry about me because I am doing well in terms of health, which is the main thing. Give lots of kisses to Papa, to Kitty and to the little girl and you, Mama, have all the love from

your little Frieda

*Self-Portrait on the
Borderline Between Mexico
and the United States*, 1932
(oil on metal)

CARMEN RIVERA
PINTÓ SU RE-
-TRATO EL
AÑO D 1932

30

4th February 1931

Dearly precious Mama

I have nothing new to tell you, but I am just sending you this letter to let you know that I am well; and for you not to worry about me. Diego has already advanced a lot in his project, and in a few days, he'll finish one of the frescoes and then he'll start another one; so, I think everything should be ready in three months. I hope it's that way so I can see you again. I also want you to tell me how Papa is doing, and how he is doing in terms of work, and if you got what I sent you.

Diego sends you lots of greetings, the same to Papa and the girl.

Mama, take very good care of yourself, try to have Chucho entertain little Isolda, that way you won't get too tired; go to the movies on Sundays so that you get a little distraction.

Don't be afflicted at all because of me, because I am happy; I am painting and besides, you can see that in a new city that one doesn't know well, everything becomes interesting and new. So I don't want you to think of me believing that, somehow, I am not doing well, quite the contrary, I am doing extremely well with everything, except that I miss you with all my heart, and although sometimes I get bored for being alone, I prefer this, because I don't like having friendships because they are a real bother. So I spend the day better when I draw or paint, instead of going up and down with idiotic old ladies or with friends who are just trying to fish some gossip. Diego is finishing his duties earlier, so he arrives at around nine or ten; we have dinner and we go to bed. Sometimes we go out on Sundays, but it's complicated because we have nothing to talk about with these dull gringos, and we just fall asleep in all the gatherings.

> "
> The gringas have liked me very much and they are impressed by the dresses and shawls that I brought with me.

Well precious Mama, kiss Papa on my behalf, the same with Kitty and the girl and you, have my entire love that you know goes from here to Neptune, or it can even be bigger.

Your little Frieda

31

12th February 1931

Dearly precious Mama

Your letter arrived at this very moment. I don't know what happened to
the letter where I sent you the banknote; I hope it didn't get lost because
we would be really in trouble. There is probably a delay because so far, no
letter has ever been lost; the thing is that the post here is not picked up
regularly from the postboxes; beg to God that the letter will get there,
because I was able to send it to you after having had a lot of jobs; it's
difficult for me to have money whenever I want; I don't have that pleasure.
However, if the letter got lost, I will try to send you more money straight
away. It's such a pleasure to hear that you all have been well. The only
thing I am concerned about is that you stay alone with little Isolda, who
ought to be devilish, but pretty, right? I wrote to Papa and to Kitty
yesterday. Poor Papa, does he have work? I tried to make crêpes already,
but they look like vomit from a drunk person, because when I turn them
around they become raw balls; it's useless for me to pretend to do any
cooking, because I don't do it well at all, I ruin everything, so I'd better
wait until I get back to Mexico so that you teach me.

Diego is doing well, working day and night like a slave, but I think he
will soon finish the first fresco. He is deciding whether we should leave
after finishing this one and he'll come back later to do the other one here
at the School of Fine Arts,[38] or whether he should paint it right away and
then we'll leave in three months. I think that although it may take him
too long, it would be better if he finishes them off in one go, because
otherwise it would be worse to come back for that later on, don't you
think? At any rate, we've been here for three months and the next three
months will pass by the same way: missing you dearly.

38
Frida is referring to the
mural, *The Making of a
Fresco, Showing the
Building of a City*, at the
San Francisco Art
Institute.

YOU ARE ALWAYS WITH ME

I am painting, I have already done six paintings that people have liked a lot. People here have treated us very well, and the Mexicans that are here in San Francisco are a bunch of donkeys, you can't imagine; however, there are idiots everywhere, and you come across some gringos that, my, they are as dumb as a brick. But they have, in general, many advantages, they are not as shameless as people in our beloved Mexico.

When I return, I'll tell you about a lot of things. You haven't told me whether Sombra's puppies are male or female; they must be adorable, right? Prevent her from messing around with another dog, because otherwise you'll have a dog school with a load of puppies and where will we end up?

Tell Kitty to ask Carlos Mérida about the money, because otherwise that old man won't do anything.

Poor Adri, she writes to me and tells me about everything that goes on, and she says she is caring for you, that way I am more at ease, because you are my only worry, Mama; you know how much I love you and I wouldn't want you to suffer at all. Tell Papa that I send him many kisses, the same to Cristi and beautiful little Isolda. San Francisco has a much better climate than when we arrived, there are flowers everywhere, and lots of sunlight, although the breeze from the ocean is always humid and my cough doesn't want to go away. My foot is already doing well and my spine is doing better, although as usual, I get tired of everything; I don't feel as sad as before and at least I am able to paint.

Listen precious Mama, tell Cristi to treat the old man very well, because I want him to buy a painting from me. Don't be bad and write to me from time to time; you can't imagine what a great pleasure I get from your little letters.

How's Uncle Pepe doing? Say hello to Grandma too.

Dear precious Mama, don't hesitate to do what I tell you, take good care of yourself, don't be alone for long, and try to go out and have fun on Sundays, even to the grimy cinema in town, because otherwise you'll get too bored; or else, take Papa to Cuernavaca on a Sunday, it costs two pesos and two on your way back, but a private car will cost you ten and Cristi and the girl and other people can go. Cristi already knows where the bus departs from; you can go in the morning and come back in the afternoon, ask Cristi to get González to take you; I'll send you the money for the fares so that at least you'd see what Diego painted at the Cortés Palace.[39]

Well my dear, I send you a million kisses and my big love. The same goes to Kitty and the little girl. The portrait of the girl you sent me looks a little bit like me and Cristi, don't you think? Take pictures of the puppies so that we can see them.

Take very good care of yourself, and in the meantime, I send you a million kisses.

Your little Frieda

39
Frida is referring to
Diego's *History of Morelos,
Conquest and Revolution*.

YOU ARE ALWAYS WITH ME

32

16th February 1931

Dear precious Mama

You have no idea how sorry I am about what happened to the letter and the money, but it won't happen to me again; I was such a fool. This week I got a letter from Cristi and Adri and they tell me you are doing well, and that's all I want to hear.

Mama, I sent you twenty dollars by telegraph, did you get it? Those were on top of the ones that got lost, and in my last letter I sent you a cheque for 150 pesos for the dogs and for general expenses; but, as I told you in the telegram, I alerted the bank not to pay them because I was afraid they could get lost again. So, tomorrow I'll send you another cheque in a certified letter.

How have you been Mama? How about Papa? Adri tells me that you end up too tired at night and that's why I don't ask you to write to me a lot, but at least once in a while, okay?

My stomach has been a little upset, but regarding the rest, my foot, my spine, etc., I am doing well. Diego didn't go to work today and we lazed around all day; he just went to the house of the Director of the Stock Exchange, they threw him a party and I didn't feel like going because of my inflammation, and it's bad to walk like that, don't you think? A few days ago I saw something magnificent at the theatre, involving African-Americans, this is what I have liked the most. The German dancers that I told you about have already left for Los Angeles, so now there is not a great deal of entertainment in San Francisco; in general, this is a somewhat sad city, because everybody works day and night, and there aren't many parties to go to. There is only one in Chinatown, where they are celebrating their New Year party, which starts in February and you can't imagine how much their parties are like the ones we have in Mexico; they set up stands exactly like the ones in Alameda;[40] they have launched

40
Alameda Central is a public park in Mexico City.

rockets for three days and they have colourful fireworks; imagine as if it were a Mexican fair; more and more I am convinced that Mexicans come from China, because we are entirely the same kind of people. The Chinese kids are exquisite, their skin is like silk and they have great similarity with the Indian kids from Mexico, but their features are finer. The girls that are eighteen to twenty-five are similar to the girls in Mexico; they dress in colours, reddish purple, yellow, etc., and the ones who dress in gringa fashion, are exactly like Mexican women: kitsch and all. They invited us, from the club of Chinese art, to attend the Chinese New Year; it'll take place tomorrow night at eight, I'll let you know how it was. That which I like a lot is the Chalet theatre, more than the American theatre, because it's really weird and they have such costumes, you have no idea; besides, the audience and the music are much more interesting.

I think that I will still not be back by the day of your saint, but I will keep it in mind from now, and I am already getting really sad. But indeed, I think that Diego will soon finish and then boom, off to Mexico!

Mama, tell me how Papa and little Isolda are doing. Tell Herminia that I am here including a little gift for her, so she'll know I don't forget her.

Dear Mama, you still haven't sent me your shoe size, so that I can buy you the Chinese sandals; don't forget (draw it on a piece of paper), okay?

After this letter, you will be receiving a cheque; you must have so many expenses, given the number of dogs, cats, parrots, etc., that you have. Has the parrot learned anything new?

Well my dear, kisses for everybody and you, have a million kisses from you daughter who adores you.

little Frieda

(I am doing well; don't be concerned). Tell Papa to write to me.

YOU ARE ALWAYS WITH ME

33

21st February 1931

Dear precious Mama

In this letter, I am finally sending you a cheque for 150 pesos, worth three months of expenses. I wish I could send you more, but you can't imagine how angry I am, because as Diego works all day he doesn't worry about money at all, and I am embarrassed to ask him for money when he comes back at home at night, all exhausted, or in the mornings, when he barely has time to get ready; so, it's very difficult that I can ask him for anything. In general, I can't talk to him too much about money, because you know that men, in general, the minute you talk to them about money they even change their tone of voice; they don't like dealing with that issue. Anyway, you understand me better than anybody else. Mama, tell me if at the end you got the letter with the money; and the other cheque too, the one I told you about, through a telegram, not to cash. Please return it to me so that I'll deliver it to Diego's own hands, that way he won't think we used it for something else; you know how much men talk. In a letter, I can't tell you about many things, but you will be able to understand.

Yesterday I received a letter from Papa and Kitty, and I will reply to them this afternoon.

I am doing well so far, my stomach got better and I am starting to eat very well again. Mama, I wanted to tell you to take very good care of yourself, the same goes to the girl, she should protect herself from a cold; you know this is hugely epidemic, try to drink a glass of rum daily, the small bottle is not too expensive; Diego says that's the best cure.

Write to me as soon as you can, because there are days when I am extremely bored and sad. I don't even know what to do, being alone all by myself. I am going to Chinatown now to see the Dragon's Parade, the one they do every year, but yesterday, like never before, I had a very boring day.

Well dear Mama, tell me how you are doing, and Papa and the girl and Kitty. We will most likely come back the first days of April; you see, it's not that long, it's the only thing that sometimes keeps me moving and takes away the sadness and boredom that I have experienced these days.

Have a million kisses from your daughter who adores you.

little Frieda

34

26th February 1931

Dearly precious Mama

I finally sent you the cheque in a certified letter, did you get it? Also, I'd like to know if you received the twenty dollars that I sent through the telegraph, because Cristi doesn't mention anything in her previous letter, and you should have got that money the following day, the day after I sent it, and I sent it almost eight days ago. The letter with the money in it got lost, right? You can't imagine how angry I got because of my own stupidity.

Mama, your saint's day is about to arrive, and unfortunately, I won't be able to be with you, but I don't want you to be sad, my sisters will tell me anyway, and if you get sad I'll be upset with you, okay? You can't imagine how bored I have been these days, as I don't see Diego throughout the day, he arrives very late and leaves very early, I am left alone and very bored; I have nowhere to go, because I already know every nook and cranny of San Francisco, besides, walking is not good for me. So, you can imagine the kind of stupid life I have. Sometimes I get tired of painting and don't know what to do. Finally, Diego will finish tomorrow his first fresco, then he'll start another one in about eight days; they have given him too much work here, but fortunately he has to go back to Mexico to finish the mural at the National Palace[41] and he can't take in many projects here; although he'll return, I already want to go back, because these dull gringos are annoying, also, the English language is very difficult, I've been here for four months and I can barely speak the basics, but when they speak fast I am at a loss. You can't imagine how difficult that damn English is. Yesterday, Lupe Luna came to see me with Alma, Rómulo's daughter, she is a woman now, such a brat, not as ugly though. Diego is going to deliver a lecture where Chavela Magaña teaches, so most likely I will see her there. She must be as obnoxious as her mother.

[41]
Frida is referring to Diego's mural, *The History of Mexico*.

Other than that, I am doing well, sometimes I just get tired because of my foot; as you know, it always hurt and more so over here, because of the ugly and ever-changing weather and because the sun almost never comes out. My stomach is doing better, and I eat very well. I haven't gone to get my injections because 'the little doctor' is not here, but he'll be back next week. I learned through Adri that Cristi finally resolved the issue with her job, I hope there is an incentive for her, don't you think? She must get desperate for not having anything to wear, etc., also, the pressure to help you out a little bit. I would like to send you something that would really help, but you know Mama, men are a pain when it comes to money, because when you ask them for money, they look as if they were pulling their teeth out; so, as much as I try, I can only send you, maybe, a little bit I take from my beloved budget, but you know it's not because I don't want to.

Precious Mama, how are you doing and what are you doing? Tell me about everything in your letters. Is the girl giving you trouble? She must be mischievous and very pretty.

How's Uncle Pepe doing? I received a letter from Carmela and she told me she had a bad cold; you dear, take very good care of yourself, because what would you do, alone and sick.

Dear Mama, I can't send you any money on your saint's day, forgive me, there is no recourse; I will send Mati a telegram because I am a little short of money.

Diego sends you lots of greetings, the same goes to Papa, Cristi and the girl.

How are Sombra's puppies doing?

Don't forget to tell me if Carlos Mérida has not made any more payments; otherwise, it's better that I send him a letter, don't you think?

Well precious Mama, don't ever forget that from time to time you need to write to me, even a little bit, because there is nothing better for me than getting a letter from you.

Let me know if Papa is out of work, that way I'll do what I can to send you some, because my worst fear is that you run out of money.

Send lots of kisses to the girl and to Cristi; say hello to Herminia and Chucho; and you dear, as always, have all my love.

Your little Frieda who adores you

(Take good care of yourself and write to me.)

35

12th March 1931

Dearly precious Mama

This week I haven't received a letter from you or Kitty, but Adri and Mati
wrote to me, and they are telling me that you are doing well so far. The
same with you, the girl and Kitty.

My foot is doing a lot better these days, the Dr returned already and
I continue getting my injections as usual, so don't worry about me, dear;
Adri tells me that you are always worrying about me and I don't want that,
if something were to happen to me or if I fell ill, I would tell you right
away, so really, you don't have to worry about me, not even for a moment.
Diego already finished his first fresco, it looks magnificent, I'll send you
pictures as soon as I can, they'll have a dinner for him the day after
tomorrow, to celebrate his first fresco. Next week we'll start on his next
project at the School of Fine Arts, my estimate is that it will take about
two months, and another month for the remaining minor projects; three
more months total and then we'll leave. You can't imagine how much I
would like to see you, without you, these months have turned into years
for me, but in no way do I want you to be afflicted because of me. I am
always worrying about Papa not having a job, or whether Cristi resolved
her issue at the university, because you can't imagine all I would do to
send you what you need, and to relieve Papa from all his sorrows for
barely making it with photography. But as you can see, it's so difficult to
say whether or not I will be able to make some money with painting,
because very few people buy paintings and above all it is extremely
difficult in this time period, but I hope I'll sell some. Tomorrow I'll send
Papa, through certified mail, the money I got by selling his photographs,
and hopefully he'll give you some money, Mama.

> "
> I go every-
> where with
> him and we
> are happy, he's
> good to me
> and he loves
> me (so far)
> very much.

Tell me how you, Kitty, Papa and the girl have been. You can't imagine all there is to buy at the neighbourhood where they have shawls, really wonderful, but you need lots of money and that's the issue. I don't know if it's better that whatever I buy for you I should send it to you little by little, or all at once before I leave, what do you think? Because I don't want to bring too many suitcases on my way back, Diego doesn't like it, we would fight during the whole trip, so I think it's better to send everything express, what do you think?

Saturday is the day of your saint, where are you going to spend it? Tell me how it went, what you did and everything, okay Mama? Adri told me that Herminia is going to marry Velador, and that was a bad surprise for me, because you'll be all alone with the girl and if you get a new maid maybe she'll be so fresh and young and she won't do any good; instead of finding a young one, I think you should get a thirty-year-old, that way she won't be that mushy, don't you think? But, anyway, it's hard to tell.

Dear Mama, tell Kitty not to forget what I asked her about my paintings.

Please tell me about everything that goes on with you; tell me if you have a monetary emergency, because I'll see what I can do and send you money right away; this is what keeps me worried, not to know about all your sorrows, etc., so please tell me about everything the way it is.

Tell Papa that I am doing everything I can to sell his collection; let's see, hopefully I can sell the whole thing.

I almost don't have anything new to tell you, because I do the same thing every day, and you know it's hard to tell you in a letter about all I see over here; there is nothing like telling you in person. I already found a Chinese dressmaker who is going to design two dresses for me, because I don't even have one, the only thing is that they charge a leg and an arm, but there is no other way, because I don't have a sewing machine and I don't know how to design them; she is going to charge me $6.50 each, let's see how they look. Let me know if you got the portrait I sent you. I am going to send you some other portraits in a few days. Write to me as soon as you can and tell Kitty to be good and to write to me too. Well Mama, send many kisses to Papa and to little Isolda and to everybody, and you dearly Mama, have all the love from your

Little Frieda who adores you

Diego sends you lots of kisses. Dear Mama: I sent Papa fifteen dollars by post, the message to pick up the money will arrive later, that way he can go and pick it up.

36

18th March 1931

Dearly precious Mama

Imagine, Diego got a telegram from President Ortiz Rubio[42] telling him that he wants Diego to finish the mural at the National Palace as soon as possible; and if Diego makes up his mind, we'll be there at the beginning of next month, at any rate, I'll send you a telegram about what is finally decided on, but first of all, I want you to tell me how much exactly the motor will cost you, as well as your house lighting installation, because you can't move without mending that; it's essential. I think the installation will cost you at least fifty pesos, and the motor one hundred and fifty, that's two hundred pesos; I'll see if I can find them and send them to you so that you can mend that immediately and in case I can't find them, it would be a good idea for you to tell Guero to get a loan and I'll pay him later, because otherwise you are going to go through a lot of trouble for not having electricity or water. You can't imagine how miserable I feel for not having even a dime to send; there is no recourse but to wait; in the event, we return right away I will not be able to do the exhibition until next year, because I don't have enough paintings. Mrs Joseph[43] wants to buy one of my paintings, I hope it's true, because we'll save the day. I don't have money to buy any of the things I wanted to bring you, because Diego has spent a lot on his assistants and everything else, so I can't asked him for money, but that's not that important, because even if I don't bring you anything, I would at least want your house to be comfortable.

In any case, Diego wants to return to the United States because he has a lot of work over here, and at least they pay him better than in Mexico, but in no way, is he getting what he deserves; we can say that in Mexico he works for alms, you know how stingy they are over there. But if he were to return, it would have to be next year because the Palace project will take time away from him; in addition, he wants to paint on canvas.

42
Pascual Ortiz Rubio (1877–1963). President of Mexico between 1930 and 1932.
43
Emily Joseph, art critic, married to Sidney Joseph, painter.

Please tell Cristi that she should find out how much it would cost to send the paintings anyway, but that she shouldn't send them until I send you a telegram telling you if I will get there the first days of April or something like that, because if we go back it's not worth sending them.

Nobody wrote to me this week; I get less letters than in the beginning. Tell Cristi not to be mean and that she should write to me often, because you can't imagine how worried I get when I don't know anything about you. I haven't been able to sell more of Papa's photographs; I sent fifteen dollars by post that I had for him; they'll let him know when they arrive; he has to check at the post office, I hope I will be able to sell more of his photographs.

Tell me how you, Papa, the girl and Kitty have been; I am doing well so don't be afflicted, and if Diego decides to leave soon, it would be just a matter of days to see each other again.

Mama, how would you think is best to do the move? In a car or in a dolly? I think it would be much better for you to do everything at once with a car, and then move the smaller things little by little, don't you think? I also want you to tell me what is it that my house needs the most, be it painting the doors or the floor or what; and I also want you to, whenever you can, buy me a piece of cheesecloth for the curtains, and have them done with Mercedes, I don't think I have spare ones; Mrs Joseph and her husband would like to come along with us, can you imagine, I need to get there and have everything ready. I also wanted to ask you if it were a good idea to hire Mrs Lola again or someone else who is more clean, because Lola is too dirty; I wish you could find one that knows how to cook, call Adri on the telephone and ask her if it's possible to find one, and another woman for the bedrooms, but don't start any of this until you get my telegram, because maybe I won't leave that soon, and will make you work for nothing.

YOU ARE ALWAYS WITH ME

I also want to ask you (a load of annoying requests for you), to get the carpenter to paint the little bars that divide the garden from the stone patio, because in white it looks too ugly. I'll send you money one of these days to have all these little things done; also, have the garden well kept. Forgive me for annoying you with all this, knowing that you are so busy, but I don't have anybody else to ask but you, because Adri and Mati do not have time for these things, and neither does Cristi.

I hope the issue with the mural at the National Palace will be sorted out soon, that way I'll know if we'll get there soon, or after Diego is finished with the frescoes he has to paint here, because afterwards it would be a matter of three or four more months and I am already desperately wanting to see you.

Tell Cristi, mainly, and everybody in general, that I would love to bring beautiful things to all of you, but it's materially impossible because I am broke, but have them forgive me.

Tell me how Grandma, Uncle Pepe and everybody are doing.

Write to me and please answer all the things I am asking you about, that way I know how the problem is going.

You will soon get my telegram so that you know if at the end we'll arrive in April or not.

In the meantime, dear Mama, send Papa, the girl and Cristi lots of kisses, and you my dear, have the love of your little Frieda, who you know loves you.

little Frieda

37

23rd April 1931

Dearly precious Mama

They finally paid me for the painting and I am sending you here three hundred pesos (one hundred and fifty dollars), so that you can mend the motor and get the lighting done, fortunately now I do think that we will very soon leave and I want you, before anything, to have your house in order so that you can move. Diego is now painting at the School of Fine Arts, but he is going to leave it unfinished so that he goes back and finishes the mural at the National Palace in Mexico City; he told me that, more or less, we'll leave on 10th May, maybe a few days later, I think, but in any case we'll be there in mid-May. I don't want Cristi to work in the next few days so that she can help you with the move and all its details etc., because it's impossible for you to do it all alone with little Isolda on top of having too many errands; so, it's absolutely necessary for Cristi to stay with you. Tell Papa not to worry at all about his office, because he can very well stay there until he wants to or while I sort out the room next to the dining room. He must know that's his house and mine. Tell Cristi that I can't send her the money that I promised, because that's all I have for now. It's not certain that I will be able to sell the other painting soon.
I think it would be a good idea to call Mrs Lola because I am going to get there and I am not going to have anybody around, don't you think? Also, she could keep an eye on the house while you move, but if you find me another woman that you think would be better and younger, that would be better. In addition, a housekeeper, but you can find one a few days before I arrive; for the cook, twenty pesos and for the other one, between fifteen to twenty pesos. If the cook is very good, I can go up to thirty pesos.

I think that most likely the house will need several restorations, but for now I will leave it like that until I get there; Mama, just get them to paint the floors with the same material they used for Aunt's Lupe's house, and get them to buy new palm straw mats; I wonder if you could order two big ones, handmade, from the mat makers, like the ones at Diego's studio, but bigger ones as they are for the dining room, and get them to paint the bathtub again. Regarding the flower pots, that would be good, but I don't know how much that would cost, including the plants, but if it's not too expensive, I can send you money in a few days. I would also like the front of the hallway in pink along with the runner, and the doors in green but like the one children use, because serious tones are too ugly (the best one is the colour of a pulque bar [light green]) and you have to warn them before they paint or else, at least the same tone, blue with burgundy, I don't know if it would cost too much, but you can ask, then just tell me in advance and I'll send you the money. Hire the mason for a set price, because you know some are thieves.

These days I haven't felt too well because of my stomach, I have just been resting without painting or anything, but I have to start packing up and get someone to clean the studio so that I leave it in good shape, I also have to do lots of other things, which will be hard on me. I'll send you a telegram the day before I leave, so that you will be absolutely certain I am coming, okay Mama?

Diego is doing well, he sends you lots of greetings, the poor thing is very good to me, I am the one who sometimes makes him wander up and down, given my temperament, which is very similar to that of a man that I know whose name is Memo,[44] but other than that everything is going well, we love each other a lot and we get along well. I have nothing new to tell you, dear, but I think that the news I am telling you about, that we are leaving, is the best one for you, right?

44
'Memo' is Guillermo Kahlo, this is what his wife, Frida's mother, would call him.

Just imagine how I feel about this!!!

Send a thousand kisses to Papa, to the girl, to Kitty and to everybody and for you, in a letter, a million kisses while I get there and I sincerely give you as many kisses as there are stars in the sky.

Your little Frieda

Say hello to Uncle Pepe, to Grandma, to my aunts, etc. I just got the letter from Papa, I will reply immediately; tell him not to worry too much for money, we'll make arrangements, motivate him and tell him that you already have money for your motor and the electricity; at least that's something, we'll sort out later how I did with the exhibition. The main thing is that you tell Cristi to stay with you this month and the beginning of May, until we get there, and tell her that it's necessary for her to help you out instead of wasting time at the university; tell her to do it for me.

38

3rd May 1931

Dearly precious Mama

I sent Adri a night letter, which most likely she already received, to tell her that we'll leave very soon; I didn't send it to you so that it would get there a day earlier, because the telegram doesn't reach the municipalities but a day later, and they don't deliver the post. Diego told me that we would leave on the seventh, but by my estimate – including leaving his job in order and the tickets, and so many other things that we need to do – we would leave after next week; that is to say, by the eleventh. In any case, I would send you a telegram two days before we leave from here so that you are certain. You can't imagine how happy I am, although I know that after four or five months we will have to come back because Diego left his job half-done, but it'll be different and lots of things that I can't write in a letter, because it's too long to talk about it.

Yesterday I received a letter from Adri and she says she is going to help you out in Coyoacán, because Cristi can only help you for two days; at any rate, I hope Kitty can ask for at least a week off, so that she can help you because it's impossible that you do everything by yourself. Mama, I am going to ask you not to incur any expenses regarding my house, because I already know you are short of money; only sort out 'the main things' needed, because you know that Diego doesn't care much and he hasn't given me money to make the restorations; I don't mean to be a pest asking him for money, and it's better that we do everything little by little when we get there. Don't you think?

Firstly, please tell me if you already received my letter with the money, because that's the main thing, and if it's enough for the motor and the lighting; if it's not enough, I'll send you the rest before departing from here; tell me honestly, because I still hope to sell the other painting, which I hope will come through; I bet you still have many issues unresolved, and that money is good for nothing. When I get there, things will be different, because we'll be able to handle money better, so don't worry. Mrs Joseph, who was going to travel with us, will apparently not leave until later, so I'll travel at ease and with no worries; hence, finding those skilful women is not absolutely urgent, you can find me an average woman for the bedroom and ultimately, Lola, who is 'really a pig' but there is recourse in case you can't find another one.

I also want you to tell me if I need to send you money for the telephone bill, my motor and the instalments, because I don't know how the issue is going (don't forget). (Write to me soon). Mama, the only thing I beg you is for you to leave the room with the idols[45] the same way Diego left it, so that there are no possible quarrels, because you know what it is he likes the most, and one must fulfil the other person's wishes, don't you think? I know you are very gentle with me and that you have all my things very well taken care of, despite all your sorrows, and you can't imagine how much I thank you (a bird told me so). I am already packing my suitcases little by little, so that I don't have to do everything at once, but as I have to do everything by myself I am delirious, because you know how clumsy I am for all that; I have to put in order all the papers for Diego,

45
Diego's Pre-Columbian
sculptures.

his paintings, anyway, many things you can't imagine; but I am pleased to do everything knowing that I will soon see you. Ask Papa if he'll be happy to see again his little Frieda who so much loves him. How are the girl and Kitty doing? You don't know how much I would love to bring them *many things* (mainly, there are beautiful things for little Isolda), but I don't have any money and it's impossible to travel with Diego with more than four suitcases because there will be a fight, for sure, throughout the trip, and I prefer to avoid that, don't you think? (I'll send by post whatever I can, because it's better that way, although it may arrive after me).

Well precious Mama, as I am telling you, I'll let you know the exact day either way. One is never certain with Diego (in terms of dates and addresses), that's why I won't believe I am leaving until I see myself sitting on the train; however, it is very certain, and I am really happy. Send a thousand kisses to everybody: to Papa, to little Isolda and to Kitty, and for you, all the love from your little Frieda who adores you.

F.

"Sometimes we go out on Sundays, but it's complicated because we have nothing to talk about with these dull gringos, and we just fall asleep in all the gatherings.

YOU ARE ALWAYS WITH ME

39

13th May 1931

Dearly precious Mama

A week ago I sent you a telegram (on the 7th), telling you that at the end we were not going to leave on that day, because Diego had not decided exactly on what date we would leave. Yesterday I sent you a night letter to Adri's address, telling you that we wouldn't leave until the following week. I haven't received a letter from any of you in more than fifteen days, maybe you stopped writing to me thinking that the letters were not going to arrive on time, but I am so anxious because of you and because of everybody, and I beg you to write to me as soon as you receive this letter. Diego received a telegram from Mexico yesterday, telling him that they will soon send him the money for the trip, so it is absolutely certain that we will leave. But, this is the issue: Diego is painting at the School of Fine Arts, and he's half-finished, if we leave without him finishing we would have to come back in September so that he finishes it; I think it's better for him to finish this project here, so that there is no need to come back because otherwise I would end up with the short end of the stick, can you imagine? I would only stay with you for three months and then I would come back here again, that would be hell. We already calculated the exact amount of days he would need to finish the mural here, fifteen days exactly, and for fifteen days it's worth staying, don't you think? In the meantime I would have to entertain those in Mexico with telegrams, and take full advantage of these last days here. So, at the end we'll arrive the first days of June; I am already and literally distraught with the change of dates and so much indecisiveness, but at least now I see more clearly, and I know that it's absolutely certain that we will leave.

Tell Cristi not to tell anybody that we'll arrive in June, because, from mouth to mouth, the news can reach those at the National Palace, and they could take away Diego's job, so it's better to say that we will arrive soon, without disclosing the date.

Mama, please write to me and tell me how your house is going, and if you have enough money, because you can't imagine how much I worry for you. I can't send you money immediately because I am short, and while Diego is working, he never remembers anything. Let me know how much I owe for the electricity, the motor and the telephone bill, because it's been three months since I last sent you money. Were you able to buy the motor? Tell me everything in detail, we still have plenty of time for your letters to arrive before I leave.

Tell me how Papa, the girl and Kitty are doing. I sent you a big package about five days ago, with several 'knick-knacks' for all of you; I don't know if it got there already. Tell Kitty that I am looking for a dress, not tailored, for her, but tell her to send me her measurements, length, hip width and bust, so that she doesn't look flat. Also, if you got the package, I want you to tell me if you got the shoes or not, because I bought them on the spot, without looking; please send me your shoe size, because none of the shoes I sent, I think will fit you. In my last fifteen days I will be able to calmly look for something for you, and for the girl, for Kitty and Papa. (Even trinkets, because I have no money.)

Tell me if your house was finished and well done, if you don't have many worries and who can take care of my house while you live in the other one. Also, tell me if you found the women and how much I have to send you for their salaries.

YOU ARE ALWAYS WITH ME

Tell Cristi to write to me, and to clearly tell me, in good hand-writing, all that has to do with money, that way I can show Diego the letter, that's the only way he would give me the money without having me pestering him for it – don't forget. But, above all, write to me. I have been very tired these days, as I thought we were going to leave on the 12th of this month, because I have been preparing the suitcases and everything, and I had the studio cleaned. Now I have to redo everything again, because during these fifteen days we have to wear the clothes again; I am telling you, it's a real pain!

Well my dear, don't forget to write to me; in general, I am well, and in terms of health too, fortunately. The Dr says that with his injections I am going to get a lot better, I don't know if you are able to understand my handwriting, but what I want is for this letter to reach you as soon as possible. Send a thousand kisses to Papa, to little Isolda and to Kitty, and for you all my love

Your little Frieda

40

20th May 1931

Dearly precious Mama

I learned that you have not been doing well because Chavela Campos wrote to me, and told me so, you can't imagine how afflicted I have been, I can't even sleep thinking about what is wrong with you. I beg you, write to me and tell me about everything that you may have. I already received letters from Adri and Mati, but as they didn't tell me you were sick, I am terribly stressed.

Mama, tell me if at the end you were able to buy the motor, because Adri tells me that you had to make new holes, and I bet the money was not enough for everything.

Diego only has eight or nine days left on his job then we'll leave; I only count the days because I am dying to see you. Tomorrow I'll send you one hundred pesos, registered post, for the telephone bill, for Salvadora's first month, and the motor; later on, I will give you money for everything you have spent on the house, Mama, because for the trip, Diego now has lots of expenses and I shouldn't be asking him for money, but later on I will get even in Mexico.

How is Papa doing in the new house? Does he like it or not? Tell him to write to me, there is still time for a last letter. At any rate, I'd like to know how you are doing; don't stop writing to me, tell Kitty not to be mean and get her to reply to me in case you can't. How is little Isolda doing? Adri also told me that she had bronchitis again. Is the new house humid? I already want to be there to put many things in order and see them, because it's impossible to think or say anything in a letter. I am really nervous and I see double, I can't even think because of the anxiety you cause me. Mama, thank you so much for everything you have done for me in the house and all. I can't even pay you for how good you have been with me, but the biggest favour that I ask you, is to take very good care of you, and to write to me so that I am more at ease. Give a thousand kisses to Papa, to the girl, and to Kitty and tell her that we'll make arrangements later regarding her job, because at the university is very difficult, and more so now that they fired López Lira.

Thank Adri and Mati for having helped me. I will write to them today. Tell Papa not to forget, and get him to write to me.

Well Mama, we will soon now see each other, I think that at the most we'll leave at the end of this month, Diego is just focusing on finishing his fresco (it looks marvellous) so that we can scram.

Did you already receive my package? In case it hasn't arrived, let me know so that I can claim it here. I hope you are doing a little better, and I am eagerly awaiting your letter.

Your little Frieda who adores you

41

21st May 1931

Dearly precious Mama

I already received letters from Adri and Mati telling me what was wrong with you. I think you should see the Dr at least once a week. You can tell him that I'll take care of the expenses for your visits, but you can't just not do anything. Precious Mama, try to eat well so that you are not weak and try not to push yourself by carrying heavy things or by exhausting yourself, because you can get a terrible inflammation. I will arrive very soon, between 5th and 6th June and I will take you to the Dr and see what we can do; in the meantime, take good care of yourself and don't work too much on the house or anything else, because if you don't take care of yourself, no one will do it for you. I am sending you here one hundred pesos to pay the telephone bills, Salvadora, the motor and the extras. I am expecting a letter from you or from Kitty so that I know what happened with the motor.

    I was very afflicted, but now that I know what's wrong with you, I think it can't be of much consequence; although you must be very careful, Dr Marín is very good regarding women's health, and I believe he will be able to cure you, so don't be concerned either, you […] [46] I wrote to you yesterday and I don't have anything new to tell you, I am just waiting for the day I board the train to go back to Mexico. Say hello to everybody, send Papa lots of kisses and to the girl and […].[47]

46
Unintelligible.

47
The original letter is ripped, and this section is missing.

YOU ARE ALWAYS WITH ME

Dear Mama, Ramón Alva,[48] Diego's assistant, is going to go to Coyoacán one of these days; he is going to pay for the lime for the National Palace project, please tell Salvadora to let him in and let him do whatever he needs to do in the back patio.

I barely have time to write to you because I have a lot of things to do before my trip. I hope you are doing better, because that's all I care about. Well dear, we will see each other very soon.
A million kisses from your

Little Frieda

Please tell Adri and Mati that I already got their letters, and that yesterday, before getting them, I sent another telegram, because I was terribly anxious but they should write to me anyway. Send one thousand kisses to Cristi and little Isolda.

48
Ramón Alva de la Canal (1892–1985). Mexican painter who participated in the Mexican muralist movement.

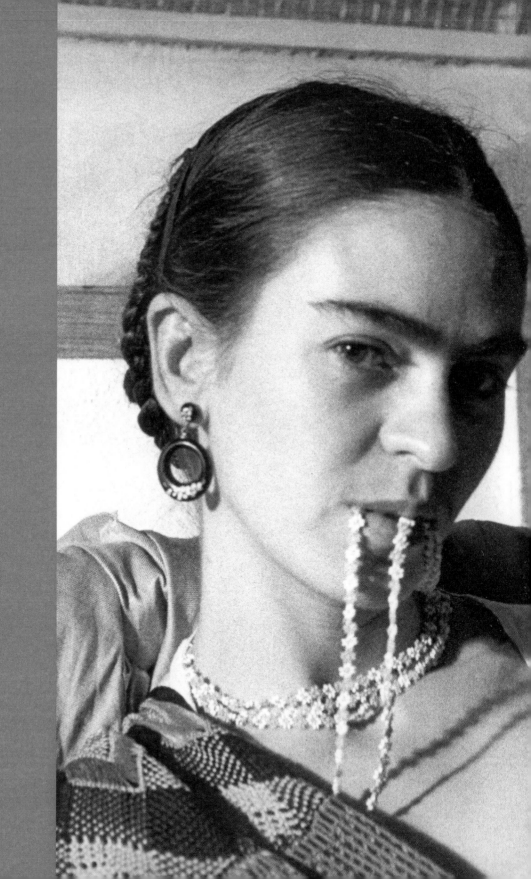

NEW YORK

AFTER FINISHING HIS MURALS IN SAN FRANCISCO, DIEGO WAS INVITED to New York where he had a solo exhibition at the Museum of Modern Art and later secured a commission with the Rockefeller family.

Frida and Diego travelled by ship, which made her seasick, but once they landed, she wrote to tell her mother that she thought she would be more at home in New York than San Francisco. Her impressions of the city were vivid, and she was fascinated by the museums and galleries. Little by little she warmed to New Yorkers, although she noted the economic disparities – America was in the grip of the Great Depression. She befriended other Mexican artists in the city: Miguel Covarrubias and his wife, Rosa Rolanda; Malú Cabrera and Ramón Alva de la Canal. The couple's social life in New York was busy; Frida found herself socialising with rich people, whom she often mocks. She told her mother that Diego was invited by Edsel Ford to paint a mural in Detroit: the *Detroit Industry* mural series at the Detroit Institute of Arts. Frida continued to miss her mother dearly and wrote that she wished she could be with her in what she called the magical city. In her painting *My Dress Hangs There* (1933) (pp.142–3) she showed her dress swinging from a clothes line against the background of a wild, wonderful and harsh New York.

ILLUSTRATION ON
PAGES 122–3
Frida in New York in the 1930s.

OPPOSITE
Diego Rivera and Frida Kahlo in their apartment in the Barbizon Plaza Hotel, New York in October 1933.

14th November 1931

Dearly precious Mama

We finally arrived yesterday, at five in the morning, in New York. I was exhausted because I got dizzy for three days straight in the boat and I felt terrible; but at least I was able to rest well last night and today I feel as if nothing had happened to me.

We live in a very good hotel with all my comforts, and on this side of the country I am doing much better than in San Francisco; the food here is also much better than in the Western part of the U. States.

New York is simply marvellous, one can barely believe this city was made by people; it feels like magic. It's so huge that looking over it from the tallest building which has 110 floors, one can barely distinguish the farthest neighbourhoods which are miles and miles away. The city is located between two very large rivers, the Hudson and the East rivers, and the view in general is magnificent. The hotel where I live is in front of 'Central Park' which is also marvellous, and in a great street and very central; one block away from '5th Avenue' where all the filthy rich live.

There is so much wealth and so much poverty at the same time, that it is incredible that people can bear such a class difference and such a kind of life, because there are thousands and thousands of people starving, while the millionaires throw away their millions on stupid things and more. Anyhow, you wouldn't be able to imagine how interesting this city is.

Dear Mama, I would like you to write to me straight away and tell me how you and everybody are doing, one by one. As I have to unpack today and do many things, I barely have time to write all that I wish, but tomorrow I will be able to explain to you everything with more details.

> "One has to have many dresses and shoes and everything; one cannot show up in rags because they will swallow you alive.

Anyway, don't worry about me, not even for a moment, because I am doing the best I can as far as the hotel goes, comforts and my health, which is the main thing. So far, Mrs Paine[49] has treated me well out of convenience; besides, I am not afraid of any of those stinky old ladies. I can almost say that I speak English and they can't fool me that easily now. Tomorrow I will write to Papa, Kitty, the chubby women,[50] Mati and Adri, and to Aunt Bela and Caro, because I have to go out to have lunch at twelve and it's already eleven-thirty in the morning. Yesterday was Diego's birthday and they honoured him with a dinner. Poor Diego, he is so exhausted, but in better spirits because he started painting right away.

You know, that which I liked about the trip was to visit Habana, it's beautiful; I will describe it to you in another letter.

Now the main thing is for all of you to write to me and to know my address, which is:

Barbizon-Plaza Hotel
Central Park South
New York

Please write to me straight away. Imagine, I lost my silver earring at the Buena Vista station in Mexico; did any of you find it?

Well dear, tomorrow I will write you a longer letter. Kisses to everybody, to Papa, the girl and everybody.

For you all my love
Frieda

49
Frances Flynn Paine, Diego's sponsor.

50
'Gordas' or 'gorditas' mean fat or chubby, respectively, depending on the context. And they are terms of endearment regularly used in Spanish.

43

16th November 1931

Dearly precious Mama

Yesterday I was not able to write to you at all, because people came over in the morning and became a hassle, and it wasn't until today that I have been able to be alone for a moment.

It's just now that I have been able to be happy, because Diego is in a very good mood and I have felt well. New York is so big that I have barely been able to get to know some of it, but little by little I am becoming aware of things.

I went to the Metropolitan Museum, and there are marvellous things there. There are paintings by the best painters; I really liked it very much, because it's the first time I see the originals by the old Italian masters; the German painters and the French modern painters. It's very interesting and one can learn many new things.

Diego is painting at the 'Museum of Modern Art' and it's located two streets away from the hotel where we are staying, so it's very easy to go there in case I need anything. I am doing a million times better here than in San Francisco, because I have everything I need in the hotel, and I don't have to do anything; the food is good and apparently, I don't have to go through the trouble of attending as many parties all the time, as it was the case over there.

You can't imagine how hot it has been here these days; it is much worse than in Cuernavaca, but they say that it can change overnight and it can start to snow. Anyway, the heat is unbearable inside the homes.

I will have to buy another hat and two more woollen dresses to go out, because the whole crowd[51] is dressed in cloth suits.

51
Frida actually uses the word 'manada' which means 'herd'. The comparison between people and animals is pervasive in these letters.

I want you to send me Hortensia Muñoz's address so that I can visit her, because she can always be helpful, don't you think?

Tell me what you have done these days; how are Papa, Kitty, the girl and Antonio doing? Tell them to write to me, my address is:

Barbizon-Plaza Hotel
58 St and 5th Ave
Central Park South
New York. USA

I sent you my address in my previous letter, but I am sending it to you again anyway, just in case something happened to the other one.

How are my aunt Bela, Caro and Romerius doing? Tell Aunt Bela that in case she needs something, she should write to me straight away.

Dear Mama, you have no idea how much I miss you and I so wish that for a period of at least three years, Diego had no need to come here. I think that if we don't go to San Francisco this year, we'll be back again in Mexico in August. Now I don't want to come back by sea, because I got really dizzy, and I don't wish this on anybody; one suffers terribly. I kept on vomiting for two full days because we encountered a storm near Habana and the ship moved more than a spinning wave and my vision was blurry. The storm was not too strong, but anyway, it was bad. Diego just made fun of me; he doesn't get dizzy at all, and he was enraptured because he was painting, but I thought I was losing my mind; Cheeta Paine gave me something and with icepacks on my head and on my stomach, I got better. I never thought getting dizzy would be so awful.

When we got to Habana it went away; we were there sightseeing for a whole day. Habana is beautiful, and it's very different from Mexico and the way I imagined it, and the people are very nice.

You have no idea how much Ramón Alva made us laugh. Here in New York he pretends to be the great connoisseur and he is very witty, because he doesn't speak a word of English, and poor thing, they get him to go up and down alone; his soul is disorientated and he is too.

I wanted to ask you if you knew what the dollar-silver peso exchange rate was, because as it goes up and down I don't want you to be short of money; tell me exactly, here I have some money which I can send you at any time, but I want to keep it until you tell me, because otherwise it's spent and there is nothing left for an emergency.

Did Aunt Bela make herself at home? Tell her that I recommend her Nahualito and the Cuerudos.

Send many kisses to Grandma and tell her that I am going to write to her. What happened to the telephone? Because I would always want Adri to keep an eye on you and to speak to you on the telephone daily.

Write to me as soon as you can, and tell me everything that goes on, because I am continuously afflicted for not seeing you.

Do you have a maid already? María, Diego's sister, told me that she would bring you one, did she?

Well dear, there is no big news to tell you, but I will write to you the day after tomorrow and hopefully I will already have one of your letters. Take very good care of yourself and don't be sad because of me, because as long as I am well, time will pass by anyway and at the end of this coming year your little Frieda will already be with you.

A million kisses. Frieda

Diego sends you many greetings, and to everybody as well. Insist with Timo to come along with you, maybe talking with her alone, without Salvadora around, she will be able to accept and she is very good; above all, it would be great for you.

Here is the list of the passengers in the ship when we came here, and the photograph of the ship so that you can keep it.

44

20th November 1931

Dearly precious Mama

You may have just received my letter yesterday, and there are still four days left for me to receive one of yours, but through Adri's and Mati's letters I learned that you were doing well, and that's why I am not that concerned. Last night we attended a concert by the largest symphony orchestra here.

The orchestra is directed by Koussevitzky,[52] who is very famous, and two hundred musicians play in it. I was falling asleep, because I don't like concerts that far away and neither does Diego, so we actually got bored. The high society here has the most stupid life you can imagine, I am terribly bored with these old ladies; I have no choice but to bear this, because they are the ones who buy my paintings; but they are the most annoying thing there is. Besides, one has to have many dresses and shoes and everything; one cannot show up in rags because they will swallow you alive.

They talk nonsense and their millions are always in their snouts. Anyway, one has to get used to everything. Today I went to the museum at nine, and I ate there all alone; there is a restaurant there for visitors; I stayed until three-thirty in the afternoon seeing everything and walking around, until my feet were hurting and I went back. There are a lot of things to see and if I don't take advantage now, later on I will not have the opportunity again. They have one of the best Egyptian art collections in the world; they have restored entire tombs they brought from Egypt, stone by stone, with very interesting bas-reliefs. They have magnificent sculptures, dating back to 4000 and 6000 BC; suits, tools, pots and pans; anyway, all the objects of the Egyptian home, objects that belong to an extremely perfect civilisation. Then, besides having antiques from Greece, dating three thousand years before Christ, they truly have marvellous

52
Serge Alexandrovich
Koussevitzky (1874–1951).
Russian director.

things, and also Christian, Roman and Etruscan art; they also have very good copies of St Mark's, in Venice and above all, with regards to painting they have the best: old paintings, medieval paintings, paintings from the Renaissance and even the modern era. They have original paintings by Goya that I had never seen before, and I am enchanted; you have no idea the way he painted, it's impossible to describe it, much less in a letter, but one can take a look at the details for hours and never get tired. There is a landscape by 'El Greco' entitled *Vista de Toledo* which is the most amazing thing in colour that I have ever seen, and many other beautiful things that I wish you could see because you would have loved them; the same with Papa. I will explain them to you in Mexico. However, after seeing Egyptian, Greek and Etruscan art, etc., the conclusion that one reaches is that there is nothing like the Pre-Columbian Mexican sculptures, it's the best or one can even say that it's the best in the world. None of these ignorant people know about it. Mexico is in fashion here now, everybody wants to go to Mexico and believe they will find the Garden of Eden. They are right in many ways, because they are already bored with this constant noise and of the anxiety in which the herd lives here. They need the air and the sun, because throughout the whole autumn and winter New York looks grey, with very fine tints of yellows and greens, but almost unnoticeable for people with no sensitivity, so they get really bored and they want to run to another place.

It's five in the afternoon at the moment, and looking out of the window there is nothing but fog; it looks as if the buildings were swimming among the clouds, because only the highest skyscrapers show their tips.

I am waiting for Diego because we are going to have dinner again with some old ladies. Yesterday in the afternoon Malú Cabrera[53] invited me to her house; obviously, to see what kind of gossip she could get, but she was very nice with me and she told me that in case I needed anything I could

53
Malú Cabrera, Mexican artist.

count on her; it's better not to have her as my enemy because she could be helpful if it were the case, don't you think?

I already walk all over by myself, because it's annoying to have old ladies come with everywhere, so I will soon, more or less, be able get a sense of direction; besides, it's very easy to find the streets here in New York, because they all go North and South and the avenues, East and West;[54] very few streets have names, most of them numbers. And I need to walk in more than one direction in the city.

I wrote to Papa, to Kitty and to everybody; tell them not to stop writing to me, the same goes to the chubby women.

You, as soon as you have time, grab a pencil and write to your little Frieda. Do you want to?

Tell Kitty that if she wants to I can send her from here a little basket for the new heir; I have seen some beautiful ones and although I may have to pay some taxes over there, it is not like buying each and everything in Mexico. But I don't know if she will want to; or, let's see what kind of arrangements we both can make.

Send many kisses to little Isolda, and greetings to Toño.[55]

Millions of kisses for Papa and Kitty and for you precious Mama, all my love.

Your little Frieda

I already have to start dressing up and that's why I can't continue writing to you, but I will write to you tomorrow.

54
In reality, it's the other way around: streets go East–West, and the avenues, North–South.
55
Antonio Pinedo Chambón, Cristina Kahlo's husband.

45

23rd November 1931

Dearly precious Mama:

Just yesterday I got a letter from Caro and another one from Mati; they tell me you are doing well, but if you can, write to me, so that I know exactly how you are doing.

So far, I am doing well, only really bored and missing you dearly. All these days have been an agony with Mrs Paine, she wants to impress us with her millionaire friends, but Diego and I laugh, and we pay no attention to her; however, for Diego, to have to dress up elegantly daily to have dinner with a bunch of thinkers, after having worked all day, is tiresome...

Everybody has welcomed us very well; the Rockefellers invited us to have dinner; the old man's son is very nice and intelligent, but, anyway, one doesn't fit in that kind of society; which, for me, is meaningless!

Miguel and Rosa, the Covarrubiases,[56] who are very good friends of ours, from Mexico, arrived yesterday. Cristi ought to remember the boy who used to go to Rosa Rouaix's house. We had dinner with them and afterwards we went to Harlem, which is the African-American neighbourhood; we went to see them dance, it was a beautiful thing, and there were thousands of beautiful mulatto girls; no one in the world dances like them, we were happy, but Diego woke up very tired today. I will have to take him to the doctor because he is very nervous and his eyes and feet get swollen; it must be his kidneys, I think, but in any case I don't want him to go on like that without healing.

The heat is unbearable in New York, it's like being in Veracruz,[57] you sweat all the time, and as the apartments and houses have little air, it's

[56]
Miguel Covarrubias (1904–1957). Mexican painter.

[57]
Mexican state and city port.

horrible. It's also necessary to have the electrical light on during the day, because the natural light doesn't come out at all. It's very annoying to live in a city like this one, because the proximity of the high-rises doesn't allow the light to come through.

Ramón Alva turned his head up to look at the skyscrapers and he got coal in his eyes, poor him, it was painful for him; I gave him Murine tear drops, and he is doing better now. Ramón is very witty; you can't imagine.

Mati told me that your telephone was working now, and I am very happy because that way you can talk to the chubby women, or you can use the telephone for whatever you want, and that would be very comfortable for you.

How is Kitty doing? And the girl and Antonio? Are you still short of a maid? Carmela tells me that Timo was going to come along with you, I hope it's true because although you may have to put up with her, you know that she was very good with me.

What is Papa doing? Tell him to write to me, for sure he must have received my letter by now.

You can't imagine how I feel about having lost my beautiful earring, I will see if I can have one made here, but it's very difficult.

Caro also told me that Antonio, the one from San Juanico, had come over; the one who has Diego's land plot, if he comes back tell him that Diego will send him money, for the instalments, one of these days. He's a good person, so don't be distrustful of him.

This is a very good hotel, but very expensive; we pay $175 dollars a month, Diego prefers to pay a little more and not be in a rat hole or far away from where he paints, and I think he is absolutely right.

Send many thanks to Guerito for the telephone, and tell him to send kisses to Chula and Carlangas and also to Gor.

Dear Mama, don't be shy and tell me if you need anything, because although they tell me you are doing well, I live with a constant fear because of you. I hope we don't have to go to San Francisco; that way, in August we will be in Mexico. Anyhow, I don't think we would stay long. I am going to draw you the apartment in the hotel so that you get an idea. [There is a drawing of the apartment on the side.]

It's located on the 27th floor, so Central Park looks beautiful from above and we have better air circulation than in other homes. The kitchen,[58] I mean, not the kitchen itself, but the electric stove, is pretty. I only make breakfast because as you know I am not any good at stewing; I make coffee, eggs – sunny-side-up style – and we eat fruit or jam or ham; this little joke costs me daily one dollar and twenty-five cents; that is, almost three Mexican pesos, which is more or less the equivalent over there.

I am going to go out now to a cheap restaurant and tonight we have an invitation; then I will have to do the same thing I do in the morning. The maid does the bed and the rest, but we have to tip and tip for everything.

As I am writing to you, I am next to the window because I have heat exhaustion.

Well my dear, don't hesitate to tell me everything and to take very good care of yourself. Send lots of kisses to the pretty and little Isolda; send my regards to Toño and tell Kitty to write to me and for Papa give him a kiss (when he is in a better mood) and don't forget that your little Frieda loves you.

Frieda

Always talk to Adri. Go and see how the house in San Angel is doing.

58
The word 'cocina' can mean both the kitchen and the stove, that's why Frida makes this distinction.

46

27th November 1931

Dearly precious Mama

I wrote you my last letter the day before yesterday, but the post takes
centuries and it's better to keep writing to you so that you are not waiting
for my updates.

I am well but very bored, as I have usually been in the United States,
but you can explain this to yourself very well.

After having had so many scorching days, it started to snow today in
the morning and it's very cold outdoors, but indoors is still terribly hot.

The park I am able to see from my window turned completely white in
a few hours, but the children go out and play anyway, as if it were not a
big deal; people don't stop going out. They collect the ice from the streets
immediately, so it only seems as if there had been a strong rainstorm.
Only the trees and the rooftops remain white.

Not that pretty, because to go out in the cold is very annoying, but
seeing the park from the window is very nice.

I tell Cristi in my letter that I haven't done anything new, and that life
is very boring here; and that only by having something to do or to read,
you can make it through here.

Diego is not very happy here and he doesn't know if we'll go back to
Mexico in January, but so far it's not certain. He has been profoundly
touched by the horrible poverty here, and by the millions of people
without work, food or homes; out in the cold and with no hope in this
country of disgraceful millionaires who have monopolised everything;
and after visiting the public dorms where they sleep like dogs in a cage,
he has started to hate this country a little bit.

Unfortunately, he has to work for these filthy rich people, but I believe
that as soon as he is done with the frescoes in Detroit, we will go back to
Mexico and stay there for a long time.

> "
> You can't
> imagine how
> different and
> troublesome it
> is for me to live
> here among
> these stupid
> people who go
> by impressions.

I haven't been able to paint because I want to see some things first, but I am going to start doing something because otherwise I will be miserably bored.

Tell me how you and everybody are doing. Don't be such a bad person, Mrs, and write to me! Adri told me that Papa has a very bad ingrown toe nail, I think Coronado can clip it with local anaesthesia, don't you think? Poor Papa, it must bother him a lot.

I feel sorry for him, because as my feet hurt so much, I don't wish the same kind of pain to anybody.

Tell me if everything is going well and what the exchange rate is for the dollar; I don't want you to not tell me anything if you are short of money. Please tell me about everything; don't ever think that Diego will read your letters and because of shame you fail to tell me what is going on.

How's Grandma doing? I also want to know if you have seen the houses at San Angel Inn,[59] because I am really interested in knowing how they are going.

It continues to snow and I am going downstairs to eat here at the hotel so that I don't go out, because I don't have rubber shoes or an umbrella. I only hope to receive a letter from you or from Kitty in order to know how you are doing. I want you all to write to me a lot.

Don't worry about me because I am doing very well; poor Diego, he's the one who is tired and bored, like me, because of the stupid life over here.

Kiss everybody on my behalf, and you dear, have my love and thousands of kisses from your little Frieda

59
Frida is talking about the home-studio designed by the Mexican painter and architect, Juan O'Gorman (1905–1982).

47

28th November 1931

Dearly precious Mama

Today I received your sweet letter; yesterday I wrote you one telling you that I was really sad because you had not written to me, but today I was so very happy to read your letter.

When I know you are doing well, I even see everything prettier than it is, and I am eager to go out and to go up and down, but when you are not doing well, I just stay in waiting for a letter from any of you.

It's already snowing very hard today, more than yesterday, everything is white already but it's not that cold.

Precious Mama, regarding what you are telling me about Uribe, I already explained in a letter to Kitty what you have to do.

I am doing very well, so far only my foot hurts as usual, but I have been able to walk well and here I found some shoes with fine leather which don't bother me at all, and they were cheap, $3.50.

I eat so so, not too well, because you know that although the food is better than in San Francisco, I don't really like it; but I eat enough food. These last few days I have gone out just a little. Last night I took Diego to see a film about Russia, which he liked a lot, and another film about ghosts, very beautiful too. Poor Diego, he needs to put his mind off the heavy load of work he has once in a while, and as he finished early, I encouraged him to go out last night.

Tonight we are going to see some paintings that Diego sold to a lady here many years ago. As you can see, one has a dull life here, but time flies and we'll arrive in Mexico with peace to stay longer.

The frescoes that Diego is painting are magnificent and I think that his exhibition will be a great success.

I would like to describe New York for you the way it is, but you know that in a letter it is difficult and I would rather tell you in person.

Regarding the pictures that you asked me about, I'll send you some that they took of us last week, I don't know how they look, but I believe they look okay.

I want you to tell me if you are still not able to find a maid, I wrote to Salvadora and I hope Timo wants to go with you.

Have you taken a look at the little houses in San Angel Inn? I would like you to go so you can tell me how the project is going. Juan O'Gorman[60] wrote to me and tells me that they have made good progress on the houses.

How is Papa doing? He has not written to me yet and I am waiting to see what he tells me about the recommendations I gave him. Regarding his mood, etc.

How is Margarita Kahlo doing? Whenever you can, go out in the afternoons for a stroll or to the cinema, don't be home bound all day, because when you see something new, you can forget a little bit your daily tribulations, don't you think? It's been a few days since I last saw Cheeta Paine, she got upset because we didn't want to spend two days with her in the countryside; I stood her up and she took it hard. Diego has to finish before Dec. 18th and he can't be wasting his time with stupid old ladies. I don't need anything from her at all, and that's what drives her crazy, that old hag.

I don't have much to tell you as I haven't seen anybody and from where I am at, I just watch the snow fall day and night. There is nothing new, and here days just go by endlessly and when we least expect it, we'll be together again. Which is the only thing I want.

Send a kiss to Grandma and to everybody.

All the love in the world for you, from your little Frieda
(Write to me whenever you can.)

60
O'Gorman designed Diego and Frida's home-studio in San Angel Inn.

Frida Kahlo
My Dress Hangs There,
1933 (oil on board)

48

30th November 1931

Dearly precious Mama

Today (Monday) I didn't get letters from any of you, and it's so awful outside that I am extremely bored. Diego left since nine and here by myself I get really bored. It's been twenty days already since we left Mexico, and it seems months to me because these cities are annoying.

My stomach hurts a little because yesterday I ate too many sweets and I am going to take Sal Hepatica.

I would like to know daily about you, but as much as I want to, it can't be; I wrote to all of you the day before yesterday and the letters may just be on their way, so it'll be a few days before I get a letter from you again, and from Kitty and the chubby girls.

Diego already finished his first fresco, it looks exquisite; he still has six more to go, and the exhibition opens on 6th December. I think we'll stay in New York throughout December, and then we'll go to Detroit. The job there is as big as the one in the National Palace in Mexico, so it will take at least four to five months, that is, until May; so if we go to San Francisco it'll be just June and July and then we'll return to New York as he'll paint a small fresco in a private house that belongs to Mrs Liebman, and then we'll run back to Mexico; at the end, it'll be September or October. In the meantime, I'll get really bored over here. The only thing I am interested in, is to learn English well, as it will be useful for me later on.

Wintertime here is very sad, the whole sky has the colour of the wings of a fly and the streets are soaked wet because of the melted snow; literally speaking, one doesn't have anything to do but to scratch one's belly.

"
New York is like Babylon, and no one knows how the rich will deal with their situation.

The rich are really scared because of the economic situation, it's getting really bad; the hotels are almost empty, all the businesses are losing millions every year, because there is no one to consume the overproduction. New York is like Babylon, and no one knows how the rich will deal with their situation, or how the workers and the unemployed will sort out theirs.

What's new in Mexico? Tell me about whatever you read in the newspapers regarding politics.

It's one-thirty now, but I am not going to go downstairs to eat because my stomach is not doing too well and I am in a bad mood; so it will be by five when I drink a glass of milk.

Yesterday (Sunday), we went to see a sculptor so that he would start a portrait for Diego, and for the first time I rode on the subway, those trains that travel underground; they travel like a bullet and you have to be quick, both when entering and leaving the train, because it only stops for a few seconds.

The neighbourhood where this sculptor has his studio is located in the east side. It's relatively close to the city centre, and there is so much filth and rubbish in the streets that you can imagine yourself being in 'Tepito' or 'Colonia de la Bolsa'.[61] The streets stink like rubbish and a bunch of dirty creatures, from head to toes, are playing around those dumps; I mean, it's horrible. Those poor people work in factories where they earn a meagre salary or else, they have to walk twenty or thirty blocks daily, twice a day, if they are fortunate to have jobs in the middle of New York.

Everything here is mere appearance, but deep down it's a real piece of dirt.

61
Working-class
neighbourhoods in
Mexico City.

I am already completely disappointed at the famous United States.

And Diego feels the same, but unfortunately he has to work here because in Mexico they won't pay him anything.

With regards to things to buy, you would get tired of all the things there are, but the only issue is to have the money to buy them. You can't imagine how different and troublesome it is for me to live here among these stupid people who go by impressions.

Have you heard anything about Galka?[62] I already wrote her a letter but she hasn't replied yet, she may not even be in Mexico any more.

Now you see, dear, I don't have anything new to say. The only thing is that so far Diego and I are doing well in terms of health, and that's the main thing.

Don't fail to see a doctor for your kidneys as soon as you can, because you know how much your feet swell, and you shouldn't stay like that. How's Papa? Tell him not to stop writing to me.

Say hello to Toño and tell him to play many piano pieces for you, that way you won't be bored; send many kisses to Kitty and to little Isolda and to my Papa.

Say hello to Chucho too.

Write to me when you are at peace, and don't forget that your little Frieda loves you.

Frieda

62
Galka Scheyer (1889–1945). German-American painter.

49

4th December 1931

Precious Mama

You won't believe it, but since the day before yesterday I haven't had time to write to you, because yesterday I went to eat at a banquet with old ladies, they were honouring Mexico and the Pre-Columbian art. Diego was not able to attend and I had to go with Paine on his behalf. The banquet took place in a hotel, that's how they do it here because the dining halls are huge; they placed a table on top of a platform and we all, the guests of honour, sat there, while the herd of rich old ladies – who paid for the banquet – sat below; they are extremely kitsch; some are over sixty years old, wearing hats with orange feathers; well, the whole crowd was a joke. Here I am, including the list that we, the guests of honours, were given! I had to sit next to the Mexican Consul, Manuel Cruz, who made me laugh all the time by making fun of the gringas; he made a speech and scolded them very well, he is very nice and intelligent. Then F. K. Rivera was introduced to the old ladies club and I had to stand up and say 'Thank you!'. And they all applauded cheerfully for meeting such a beautiful and important person. We left the place after we ate and I went to see Diego with Cheeta Paine, then around seven we went out to have dinner at a Mexican restaurant. I swallowed three scrumptious chicken tacos with green chilli pepper and fried beans. They played Mexican *corridos* for us and we left at nine and we even went to talk to Cheeta until eleven or midnight; when I arrived I was so exhausted that I couldn't write to you or anything.

Miss Dunbar, who went to Mexico, invited me today to have dinner. She is the gringo's wife for whom Diego painted a big portrait, remember? Well, we went to a restaurant that they call a 'speakeasy' here; because it's where you can find all kinds of wine, whichever you like despite the ban. From the outside you can't really see there is a restaurant, but when you walk in, through a little hall, sort of intricate, you reach a huge room where there are more than one hundred and fifty tables full of people. They have an orchestra with five or six musicians and as everything is closed, there are no windows facing the streets and everybody smokes; it's hell in there, and I felt that my feet were collapsing and that my head was spinning due to the noise; also, the musicians not only play but also sing and they don't do it too well and the cigarette smoke, which is the only thing you breathe in there, plus whichever wine or cocktail you drink, will drive you crazy; literally, you speak and the person who is next to the constant noise can't hear you. Besides, the walls are decorated with mirrors and they are placed in such a way that they give the impression you are looking at the room from everywhere; as if you had eyes in your feet, in your back, and on the top of your head; but the impression that you get is that you get an immediate and terrible headache and you feel like vomiting, that's all! Each day I understand less and less these ignorant people; they spend their money on such stupid things that no one else would think about; imagine, spending two hours in a restaurant like that, with the air full of smoke and such people; well, only an idiot could think of that, don't you think?

I finally left that madhouse and took to the streets and walked in the middle of a snowfall that was taking place in the afternoon, because that was the only way for me to breathe some air, because if you hop in a taxi, it's like a stove. But my headache continued and I came back to the hotel to sleep a little, now that I woke up it is six-thirty already, I fell asleep straight away for two and a half hours.

I would like to tell you more but that's generally what I have done these days; I have been happy because last Monday I received a letter from Caro; on Tuesday one from you and Mati. Yesterday, one from Adri and Papa, and today one from Kitty and Paca Toor.[63]

63
Frances Toor (1890–1956).
American author.

I would love to reply to you all now, but I have to go to the shop and buy something to eat for Diego, because poor him, he doesn't eat lunch and he arrives at night very hungry, and I want to go immediately because later on I feel terribly lazy, so tell everybody that I will write to them tomorrow. This morning I only put in the mail a letter for Kitty, and I included a cheque for you to pay Magaña, Antonio, the one from San Juanico, and have the motor fixed, and to pay the Ericsson telephone.

Dear, tell me how you are doing; tell me many, many things; send little Isolda lots of kisses and talk to her about me so that she doesn't forget me. Send many greetings to Toño and Kitty, and kiss my Papa for me, I'll write to him tomorrow.

Don't stop writing to me, and don't worry too much about me, because I am doing well, the only terrible thing is that I am not with you, but time flies like a bullet …

Your Frieda

50

13th December 1931

Mama, forever in my heart

I miss you more each day, and I have no choice but to wait until time passes by. I have received letters from everybody and at least I am happy because I learned you are doing well. Fortunately, I haven't even got a cold and Diego is very tired, but doing relatively well in terms of health.

Everything is the same over here, terrible weather, and life doesn't have much purpose. But anyway, it's good to get to know about everything and there is always something new to see and to learn from everywhere you go. Mati told me that she saw you last Saturday and that you were very happy at the villa; I am so sorry I wasn't there, the party must have been delightful with so many people around.

Despite there being more people here than there should be, people barely see each other because everything is so big, that they look like ants next to a hill.

Diego's exhibition will soon open and I think it's going to be magnificent, because his frescoes are exquisite. Poor him, he works so much and sometimes I even get scared he could become ill.

I have been to the cinema, and to the best concerts they have in New York; some are a disgraceful, but the last one I attended, had a famous director called Stokowski;[64] it was marvellous.

Last night we had dinner with Malú Cabrera, we had Mexican food. We took Ramón with us and he ate so much that he must have diarrhoea today.

It's horrible outside today, and it's almost like this every day, cloudy and bereft of colour; I am not in the mood for anything, just to lie – belly down – because I am really bored. There are neighbourhoods in New York which are much more interesting than where we live, but they are too far away and as you know, due to my leg, I am not able to walk too

64
Leopold Stokowski
(1882–1977). English
conductor of Polish and
Irish descent.

much, just around here. Taxis are really expensive and one spends like crazy for whatever little thing you want to do.

Is it true that there are already new banknotes in Mexico? Tell me what they look like and how everything is going over there. Obviously, it must be really bad like everywhere else.

I wrote my last letter to Cristi the day before yesterday; I don't know if she will get it later, because I sent it registered.

Tell her to write to me, I am always thinking how she's doing, and I am uneasy because of her. How's Guero Veraza[65] doing? Mati tells me he had influenza, is it true?

How about the girl? Tell me what she's doing, if she's able to speak fully and if she's as pretty as I last saw her.

Send many greetings to Toño on my behalf.

I also wrote to Papa, so expect that I will soon get a letter from him.

I rather not tell you too many new things, but to continuously write to you instead, that way there is nothing pending from me and you won't worry too much, don't you think?

We already got the receipt for the idols that Kitty sent. Dear Mama, you have no idea how much I thank you for all you do for me, you are so sweet, because after dealing with all your troubles, you still have more to deal with regarding everybody, but that's the only way things can turn out well, don't you think?

Write to me, whenever you see Aunt Lupe, tell her that I congratulate her with many kisses. It's been more than a month since we are here; you can see how fast time passes by, the least you expect it, we'll be together again. Take very good care of yourself so that your

little Frieda, is happy

65
Alberto Veraza, Adriana Kahlo's husband. From his previous marriage, Veraza had a son, Carlos (Carlitos/little Carlos) Veraza Uthoff.

51

18th December 1931

Dearly precious Mama

Yesterday I was very happy because I got four letters, one from Cristi,
Papa, Mati and Adri, all at once; they all say they are doing well, and that's
the only thing I want. Besides, today in the morning I got Mati's letter
where you wrote to me a little note, and I was very happy about it; you
can't imagine how much. Here everything is going well; when I come
to the United States I get really skinny, but I don't feel ill, most likely it's
the weather that doesn't suit me or I don't know what it is, but that's not
that important.

Poor Diego, he is literally exhausted. You can notice it by looking at
his face, and he's in a bad mood these last few days because the old Mrs
Paine has done some stupid things regarding the arrangements of the
exhibition, framing, etc. and those things drive Diego crazy, and he is
absolutely right, because after working like a dog he has to take care of
details after details and that old lady could very well take care of them,
don't you think? Anyway, the exhibition will open on the 22nd, I will send
you the invitations and a catalogue so that you see it and keep it.

I do nothing, just mess around; my days here go by so quickly, and at
four in the afternoon New York is pitch black like a wolf's mouth;
sometimes I go to the cinema, I have two close by, in one of them you can
only watch 'world news', that is, a kind of review of what goes on
everywhere and in the other one, sometimes the films are good, but other
times just rubbish. I like going to the cinema because I can listen to the
films in English, and I can practise.

> "
> Despite there
> being more
> people here
> than there
> should be,
> people barely
> see each other
> because every-
> thing is so big,
> that they look
> like ants next
> to a hill.

In terms of plays, I haven't seen anything great, but let's see if I go next week; but you know what, I get bored because I can't ever count on Diego, and I don't have anybody I can trust; I am alone all day and very bored, at the same time, I'd rather be alone than having too many friendships, because they are costly and they are only good for bothering you.

Tonight I am going to go to see a lady, who is very nice, and who is the wife of a literature professor at Columbia University. She speaks Spanish better than me, even though she is a gringa, because she speaks it as if she had been born in Madrid; she learned in Spain and with her husband who is very intelligent and famous as a linguist.

The other day, this same couple, invited me to have tea at their house; they have a four-year-old boy, the most beautiful thing you can imagine; really intelligent and he speaks Spanish and English fluently, we got along very well, and since I arrived early and that lady was late, he played with me, he eagerly showed me all his toys, I was reminded so much of little Isolda that I was almost crying St Peter's tears! But I held myself. Well, you can't imagine how beautiful that little boy was, a little chubby, and he spoke like an adult about everything. At night that lady and I put him to bed, she would ask him, 'Little Juan, do you want water?' And he would reply, 'No!!' His mother kept on asking him about many things, and he would reply 'no' to everything, and then he goes: 'Listen mother, do you know what I want, what I want is for you not to bother me so much, and for you and this madam to go away and let me sleep alone!!' Well, you can't imagine how funny this little boy was!

I don't have any other news, because you can see that I have a silly life here. I have gone once to the theatre by myself, it's very good, and I liked it more than the dramas and tragedies of the French theatre; here it is simpler and done more naturally.

I started this letter yesterday and I am still writing it this afternoon, because I haven't had time for anything. Today in the morning we went to see the Indians from New Mexico; they came to have an exhibition of their paintings, fabrics, sculptures, etc., and they danced some sacred dances that were very pretty; they all speak Spanish like the Indians from Mexico, and they are almost identical, the only thing is that these Indians have not racially mixed with any white race, while in Mexico they are already spoiled. They were delighted to talk to us, and straight away they treated us informally, as if they had known us since a long time. They are very intelligent and they paint beautifully.

Diego got into a better mood while talking to them, because all these days he has been very upset, and he is absolutely right; imagine, as you already know, that he painted five frescoes for the exhibition, he painted them over a flat lime surface, using sand and marble dust which they prepared in an iron frame, like this one[66] with fabric made out of wire.

Well, the framing was not done right nor was it strong enough to withstand the flat surface. Besides, he painted them on the sixth floor of the building, where the exhibition will take place and when he finished, they had to bring them to the twelfth floor and naturally, it's a lot of work to bring upstairs, through the narrow elevators which that building has, something that heavy and delicate at the same time. Well, to make a long story short, they ruined the edges of five frescoes, and they scraped two figures on the lower side; all this, because of Mrs Paine's stubbornness and stupidity, because she insisted that Diego should paint on the sixth floor, and she is the one who ordered such weak framing, and all the crap

66
Frida draws her a canvas.

she's done. Imagine how furious Diego was, he was pulling his hair out because of his rage, and he wanted to leave as soon as possible; finally, today in the morning he got his mind off things, and I took him out to eat and to take a little stroll and he got better, but he is right because after so much work they have done shabby work; Ramón is now going to redo the parts that were scraped and I think they will look good.

Dear Mama, I have wanted to write to Cristi since yesterday and I haven't been able to, the same goes to Papa, so don't ever think that it's because I am lazy; but indeed, there are days that I can't do my things, because the old ladies annoy me with their invitations since very early in the morning and I can't do anything about it.

I already got the receipts Kitty sent me, tell her that I am very thankful, and to reply to the letter I sent her four days ago about the clothing we spoke about.

This letter already looks like *El Universal*[67] but I wish I could write to you all day, but these bad people don't let me.

How was the party in Villa de Guadalupe?

Send many kisses to Papa, to Kitty, to the girl and to Toño,[68] and tell them that I will write to them tomorrow at the latest, because I have to go out with a gringa to see a Picasso exhibit.

Write to me dear, whenever you can, and have the whole heart of your little Frieda who adores you

I will also write tomorrow to Adri, Mati, Caro and to everybody.

67
Mexican newspaper.
68
Antonio Pinedo
Chambón. Cristina
Kahlo's husband. His
nickname was 'Toño'.

52

26th December 1931

Dear Mama

Your letter arrived right at Christmas, and I was happy all day to learn that you were doing well. I wanted to reply to you yesterday, but I couldn't because we were out all day.

On Christmas Day Diego worked until eight-thirty at night and I stayed at the hotel because I didn't have anywhere else to go, but Malú Cabrera invited us to have dinner at her house on Christmas Eve; we had baked pork and salad, it was delicious. You have no idea how much I remembered you, because do you remember the delicious salads you used to make during Christmas Eve? We had a good time, only Rosa and Miguel Covarrubias, Malú and her husband, two brothers-in-law and Ramón Alva came over. Malú decorated her Christmas tree and set up her nativity set; she also set up a Christmas tree for her cat, which is beautiful; a really beautiful Persian cat. After dinner, they gave away the presents, they gave me a very beautiful green necklace and Rosa Covarrubias gave me a red and green cravat, very beautiful too. Diego got a wallet of fine leather and Ramón got a handkerchief.

We were singing with the guitar – only Mexican songs, and I only thought of you all, of you above all. Poor Malú, she did all she could to make us happy and at two in the morning we went to Remo Bufano's house, the Italian sculptor, and we continued singing and making noise until four in the morning, when we went to bed; they all toasted for 'Mrs Rivera' and they treated us well, and they were all humble people, trustworthy, and not the stupid rich people.

Cristi must have told you already that I fought with the hag, Paine; to be nice with me, on the 25th, she sent me a flower pot for Christmas, and she went to see Diego to ask him exclusively about me, but I have not paid any attention to her, and I barely say good morning and goodbye to her; don't you think that's the best thing to do? Since early in the morning, the 25th was all about getting Christmas cards and presents; Mrs Rockefeller sent us a bouquet of flowers on Christmas Eve. From San Francisco, Emily Joseph sent me a very beautiful golden match box, with my initials on it, and to Diego, a box of very fine sweets. The Josephs are very nice people, she is the lady I told you about who was very nice with me in San Francisco. The rest of the people here in New York, gave us books and things to eat; many things on Christmas Day. That is, the party is on the 24th at night, but they still do something on the 25th; that day the Oníses invited us over to have dinner, they are the ones I told you about who are very nice; he is Spanish and she is American, but she speaks Spanish better than me. Diego really overate; he had rice, Valencia style, and baked turkey; the food was good and we were happy about it. On the 25th at night we went out with a young gringo who lived in Mexico for three years and who knew Diego. He took us to an Indian restaurant, I didn't even try the food because I don't like being so 'exotic' in terms of food, because I can suffer a tragedy right there at the restaurant. But Diego ate like eight madmen, and he loved Indian food; there were some beautiful Indian women; there was one who looked like Kitty, she was only a little darker, but the same type.

Then from there we went to a kind of cabaret, where a Mexican couple were going to dance 'Jarabe Tapatío'; they didn't dance it well because the girl wasn't Mexican but Indian and Chinese, and he was a brat without any charm; but they were nice people; the gringo who took us over there introduced them to us. I was already exhausted watching gringas who were half-naked dancing silly dances; they were so dull that they looked like dancing onions; they looked so horrible being not only blonde, but also almost albinos; scary!!!

We went to bed at five in the morning, I was literally exhausted, but you know how men are, they never get tired and Diego and the other man were as fresh as if they had just come in. Anyway, we weren't so bored during Christmas and life has come back to normal, Diego working and I... doing just NOTHING.

Mama, tell me what you all did; imagine, no matter how hard I tried to send little Isolda's clothes so that they would arrive on the 3rd, I wasn't able to because during these Christmas days the shops are literally full of people and I have been dealing with Diego's exhibition, meeting people and more people, who bother me all day; so today I'll send her clothes in the afternoon, even though they may arrive later than on the 3rd. How much I would love to travel along with those clothes!

Today I got a letter from Papa, as funny as usual, but typically he complained about life; I suggested he should start painting and stop working at least for two months, what do you think? I'll send him money for whatever he needs: cigarettes, sweets, etc., and that way he would be more calmed, don't you think? But most certainly, he must not want to. Ask him, in case he does.

Mama, please send me Mr Hale's address, because he sent us a telegram and I'd like to reply to him. Don't forget it. Diego's exhibition has been a success; each day two to three thousand people go to see it, and most of them love it; he's painting three more frescoes, and afterwards he has to do two portraits and then we'll go to Detroit. Hopefully it won't occur to him to go to San Francisco, that way we'll be back in Mexico between the end of May to the beginning of June; beg God that's the case, because these five months will pass by quickly. I'll let you all know the day we leave New York.

Please tell me how you are doing and how is Kitty and everybody doing; take very good care of yourself. Say hello to Grandma and give lots of kisses to the girl the day she turns three; she ought to be gorgeous.

I am doing well so far, the same goes to Diego, so don't worry.

I hope the new year is better than this one for everybody, and I hope that we'll soon be together for ever. Mama, don't stop writing to me and telling me whatever happens to you.

Kisses for everybody and for you all the love from your little Frieda

I am going to send you the catalogue of the exhibition.

53

8th January 1932

Dearly precious Mama

Today I received a letter from Kitty, she says that I shouldn't be that lazy and that I should write to you more often; but you won't believe it, there are weeks in which I don't even have time to scratch myself; there are people bothering me with invitations during the day, in the afternoon and night. And at night I am exhausted from going up and down. And this week, after the exhibition opened, it has been one of the worst, because everybody wants to invite Diego for tea, dinner or a party, and the occasions for which he is not able to attend, I have to go in his absence. He has delivered two beautiful talks, one at Columbia University and the other one at the Public Library in New York. People liked them. It's useless to tell you about the rest of the dinners, etc., because they are all boring and annoying.

More and more people see the exhibition each day. In nine days, nineteen thousand people have seen it. They say that there has never been an exhibition like that in New York.

Diego is now painting portraits, and we are going to stay here throughout January; then, according to Diego's plans, we'll go to Detroit. But, it was published in the newspapers that the museum in Detroit, where Diego has to paint, sacked its director along with its employees, so it's not too certain that we'll go there. I am very sorry, because Diego was really enthusiastic about painting *The Steel Industry* over there, and feel sorry that his wishes wouldn't come true; but, on the other hand, it would be much better, as we would return to Mexico much faster. Anyway, who knows how the museum contract will turn out, at any rate, I'll let you know in advance where we will go in February.

> "
> At four in the
> afternoon New
> York is pitch
> black like a
> wolf's mouth.

YOU ARE ALWAYS WITH ME

Mati tells me in her letter how beautiful little Isolda looked with her 'china poblana' dress, dancing to 'Jarabe Tapatío'; when I read Mati's description I was screaming, remembering you and the girl and everybody, but I know I have to wait because there is no other way around.

Dear, tell me how you and Papa are doing. Fortunately, I am doing well in terms of health; I am tired of this life among presumptuous and idiotic old people, but at least I keep Diego happy, he is painting and painting all day, and apparently, he is doing well and he hasn't become ill or anything. Time will pass by quickly and we'll return to Mexico as soon as possible. In terms of money, everything is really bad here. So far nobody has bought anything at the exhibition, but I hope that later on people will become interested in the frescoes, because this trip has cost Diego a lot, and hopefully he'll have good sales, otherwise, it would be terrible, don't you think? My biggest worry now is Kitty, but I think that if she takes good care of herself everything will turn out okay. She says that Marín is charging her $250.00 pesos, that's far too much, don't you think? I don't think it is fair he charges that much. I'll see if Diego is able to write him a letter or I myself will write him one telling him not to overcharge her, but in case we are not able to do anything, I think that other doctors may charge her less.

I didn't send her the little basket, because the Mexican consul from here suggested that he could bring it to Mexico in March, so I decided to send her the money instead; that way she can buy her things over there. I already sent, although very late, little Isolda's clothes, so they'll get there on the 13th of this month; as much as I tried, I was not able to send them before.

The weather in New York changes overnight; some days we can have sleet and other days a nice hot day, but in general, it's cold at night. Is it too cold in Mexico?

I am going to write a little note to Lupe Paul because of what they underwent with their child, poor little Manuel, he ought to be desperate!

Dear Mama, if you can, write to me at least a little, little letter, do you want to? You can't imagine how much I love your letters.

Malú Cabrera is the one I see more often, she has been nice so far, I know she is fake, like a one-cent coin, but anyway, at least she speaks Spanish and I have someone here just in case, don't you think? Besides Malú, I see Rosa and Miguel Covarrubias, who are very good people.

I have another American female friend, who is more or less my age, and I get along with her because she is simple, not pretentious and a good person; her name is Wilma Carmon. Next month she'll travel to China, because she is going to marry a fellow who is the consul in China, and her father will take her and walk her down the aisle. She is very witty and cheerful. She's not pretty but she is a good person. I almost never see the hag, Paine, and when I see her we barely talk. I don't trust her at all and I don't like her.

There is nothing new. Everything is the same and I like New York more than in the beginning, but the only thing I want is to go to Mexico and see you.

Send many kisses to Papa, to Kitty, to the girl, to Toño and to everybody, and you dear, have a thousand of kisses from your little Frieda who adores you.

F.

Send me little Isolda's picture with the 'poblana' dress. Don't forget it and also Hale's address.

54

14th January 1932

Precious Mama

Yesterday in the afternoon I received your letter, I wanted to write to you in the last four days, but I had a bad cold with a really bad headache, and I had no desire to do anything. I was better yesterday in the morning and I went out because it was very hot inside the hotel and there was a nice day out; I still have a sore throat and I feel a little deaf and cold-sick, but at least I got better; I was scared that I could have a lung complication or something worse. I have taken good care of myself and this is enough to prevent any bad thing. You have no idea how bored I was during those four days that I stayed in the hotel, because when you don't feel well nothing is fun. Lots of people came over to see me and they sent me flowers, etc., etc., all this bothers me more than a kick in my stomach, but I have to put up with this. Malú Cabrera comes to see me daily, the same with Rosa Rolanda and other girls that I have met here; I am so bored and out of the mood, and there is no recourse, even though they have tried to entertain me. It must be because I am alone, because in the first place I can't count on Diego for a lot of things; he doesn't cease to paint or to deal with things related to his work, not even for a moment, so sometimes I don't even have time to talk to him about things that I would like, because I never have a chance. He leaves early and comes back late tired and only wanting to sleep. Anyway, I live life alone and my soul is alone, because I hate all the friendships I have for being obnoxious and pretentious people.

And when you are sick you can't trust strangers, so I prefer to set up things myself and to do everything by myself, as there is no recourse.

And it's not that Diego doesn't care, but, in the first place, in these cases men are really useless, and in the second place, they are not aware of what is happening to women, don't you think? And they think everything is 'nothing' as long as there is nothing happening to them, but if it were happening, the world would crumble.

Fortunately, I can say I am doing better already, because the only thing I have is a cold, which should go away in two or three days.

Dear Mama, you don't tell me in your letter how your feet are doing or if they still get swollen as before; I would like for you to heal permanently, that way your kidneys would have a long rest. Diego is also suffering from his kidneys and I don't know what to give him, because he doesn't want to go and see a doctor.

Regarding what you are telling me, that Pinedo and Cristi would like to move to another house, I find that very difficult at this moment, because with Kitty's upcoming issues and being alone in another house it would be the same as the other time and, on the other hand, you wouldn't have that big a responsibility and it would be better for everybody. But I don't think that they would move without being completely sure that they will be able to support, by themselves, a household.

In case this were to happen, I would be the only one ready and you would move with me to my house in San Angel Inn. We would rent the other houses, or we would see what we would do, but in any case, if Cristi wants to move alone to her house, you will come with me and with nobody else. The advantage in San Angel Inn is that I will live in my house and Diego would live in his,[69] and if you and Papa were to move in with me, I would love it. Just let me know in advance about whatever Cristi and Antonio decide, that way I'll see how everything gets resolved.

I think that on 5th February we'll leave from New York to Detroit; Diego believes that his project will take approximately from three to four months, then, if we don't go to San Francisco, we'll return to New York for another commission that he has over there, and we'll then return to Mexico. But if while being here, Cristi and Antonio decide on something definite, let me know because I'd like to know what we would do right away.

Because I don't like it that you stay at home by yourself. I don't want you to. Likewise, I don't want poor Papa to worry about anything else; and I want for the two of you, including myself, to live very happy and without any worries.

Poor Diego will fall in love with his house in San Angel Inn, he'll paint all day, and we would be in the other house without bothering anybody, and nobody would bother us, don't you think?

Write to me and let me know about everything that goes on; especially, tell me how your feet are doing.

Did little Isolda's clothes arrive? I sent them from here on the 5th, it's enough time, they should have arrived already. Please let me know, I would also like to know if Cristi got the letter with the cheque, because I didn't send it registered post. Dear Mama, take very good care of yourself, and beg

69
Juan O'Gorman designed this as two separate houses connected by a bridge at the top.

all the saints so that I return to Mexico soon. Here I am just among really obnoxious old ladies and I don't even see a ray of light, and the food is like vomit for me; I hate everybody here except for the military personnel and the children younger than four years old, and the rest, particularly the 'old ladies', they are worse than a season in hell; they are terrible and idiots. Dear Mama, I am sending you this letter to Adri's house, because I don't want to blunder regarding the arrangements that Cristi and Antonio may have, as they haven't told me anything. That way, Adri will deliver this letter to you directly in your hands, and you will be able to read it at your leisure.

Write to me dear, whenever you can. Don't worry believing that I am ill or anything, because I am telling you, I just have a cold and when it's gone in two days, I'll be completely well.

Send many kisses to Papa and to everybody and you have a thousand kisses from your little Frieda who loves you

> " Diego's exhibition has been a success … in nine days, nineteen thousand people have seen it. They say that there has never been an exhibition like that in New York.

EPILOGUE

Matilde Calderón Kahlo died from cancer on 15th September 1932. Possibly she knew her death was not far off as she wrote in her beautiful even script – unlike her daughter's handwriting – to Frida in January of that year, 'I would do anything to travel with this letter to where you are, and kiss you and talk to you ... I hope we'll soon be able to do it.'

A few days before her mother's death, Frida, who was also bearing the grief of a recent miscarriage, had travelled home from Detroit where Diego was painting his Detroit Industry mural series. As well as sharing letters, we know they had been able to speak to each other as in a letter dated 15th August 1932, Matilde wrote of her joy after a telephone conversation. 'My charming girl: I will never be able to explain to you the deep feeling I got when I heard your voice, so clearly and so well that it seemed you were next to me. I thanked God and the man who discovered the power to speak at such a long distance ... whatever I say would not be enough to express that feeling I had for the first time in my life.'

She signed her letters, 'Your mother who adores you, Matilde'.

A month after the death Frida returned to Detroit and, significantly, completed *My Birth* (1932). She wrote in her journal that it depicted her giving birth to herself and of course we cannot help but wonder about her sadness at not being able to have her own children and about her memory of her mother. Like almost all of Frida Kahlo's work it demonstrates the birth of a new aesthetic and both the pain and the commitment to life.

Frida continued to paint until her death. She died in Coyoacán on 13th July 1954.

OPPOSITE
Frida around the time
of her mother's death,
photographed by her
father in 1932.

YOU ARE ALWAYS WITH ME

I wouldn't have been able to publish this book without the support, help and assistance of Ruth Gross (North Carolina State University), Jennifer Page; Sarah Osborne Bender (National Museum of Women in the Arts), Maria Elena Gonzalez Sepulveda (Frida Kahlo Museum), Jose Antonio Lopez Martinez; Carla Barri Rosendo (Bank of Mexico), Lynn Miller (National Humanities Center) and Lennie Goodings (Virago Press), and I thank them all wholeheartedly. Also, the support and love of my mother Ana Matilde, my sister July and Mariela, my wife; they 'were always with me' and I thank them from the bottom of my heart.

HÉCTOR JAIMES

IMAGE CREDITS

Front cover and frontispiece © Bettmann/Getty Images

Pages 6–7 © Fine Art Images/Heritage Images/Getty Images

Page 11 Private Collection/Photo: Jorge Contreras Chacel/
Bridgeman Images

Pages 16–17 The Museum of Modern Art, New York/Scala, Florence

Pages 18–19 © Granger, NYC/TopFoto

Page 22 Art Collection/Alamy Stock Photo

Pages 30–1 Museo Dolores Olmedo Patino, Mexico City, Mexico/
De Agostini Picture Library/G. Dagli Orti/Bridgeman Images

Pages 36–7 Detroit Institute of Arts, USA/Founders Society Purchase/
Diego Rivera Exhibition Fund/Bridgeman Images

Pages 47 and 65 The Nelleke Nix and Marianne Huber Collection:
The Frida Kahlo Papers. Special Collections, Library and Research
Center, National Museum of Women in the Arts

Pages 51 and 176 Pictures from History/Granger, NYC

Pages 88–9 Private Collection/Photo © Christie's Images/
Bridgeman Images

Page 111 San Francisco Museum of Modern Art, San Francisco
© Banco de Mexico Diego Rivera and Frida Kahlo Museums, Mexico,
D. F./Artists Rights Society (ARS), New York. Photograph: Ben Blackwell

Pages 122–3 Photography by Lucienne Bloch (1909–1999)
Courtesy Old Stage Studios

Page 125 CSU Archives/Everett Collection/Bridgeman Images

Pages 142–3 Private Collection/Photo © Christie's Images/
Bridgeman Images

Page 171 Granger, NYC/TopFoto

YOU ARE ALWAYS WITH ME

Héctor Jaimes is professor of Spanish at North Carolina State University, USA.

"

I just wait for your
letters because that,
and having Diego,
is the only thing
I care about.